GRANUAILE
Queen of Storms

Dave Hendrick

Illustrated by Luca Pizzari

Colouring by Dee Cunniffe

Lettering by Peter Marry

THE O'BRIEN PRESS
DUBLIN

For Marion, for safely guiding me through all the
storms that have come my way.
Thanks, Mom.

Special thanks to Luca for his vision, to Dee and Pete, for
giving us exactly what we needed at precisely the right time,
and to Helen, Emma and all at The O'Brien Press for pulling
this all together.
Dave Hendrick

To Dee, for the help;
to Dave and Helen, for the trust;
to Luisa, for the patience.
Luca Pizzari

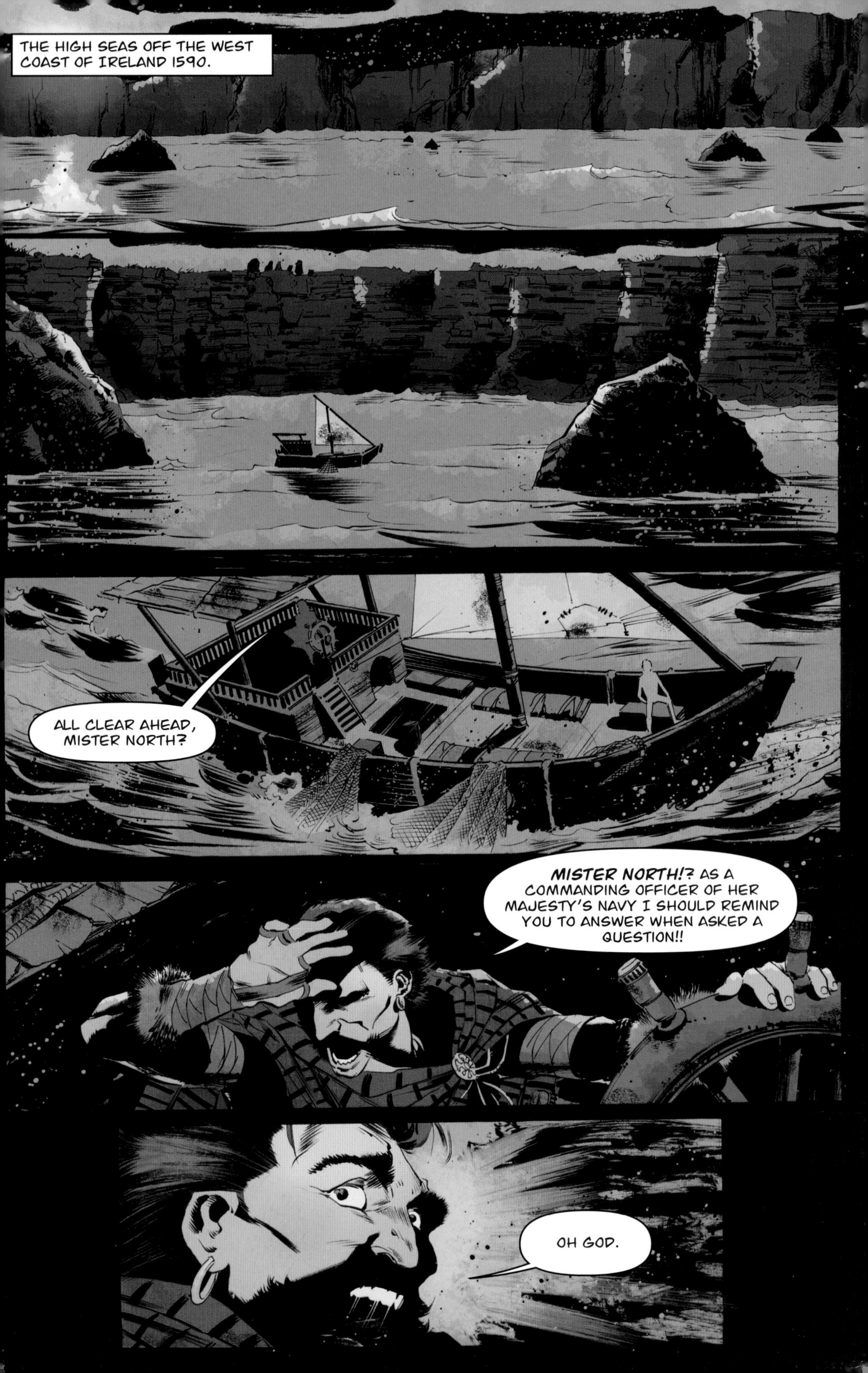
THE HIGH SEAS OFF THE WEST COAST OF IRELAND 1590.
ALL CLEAR AHEAD, MISTER NORTH?
MISTER NORTH!? AS A COMMANDING OFFICER OF HER MAJESTY'S NAVY I SHOULD REMIND YOU TO ANSWER WHEN ASKED A QUESTION!!
OH GOD.

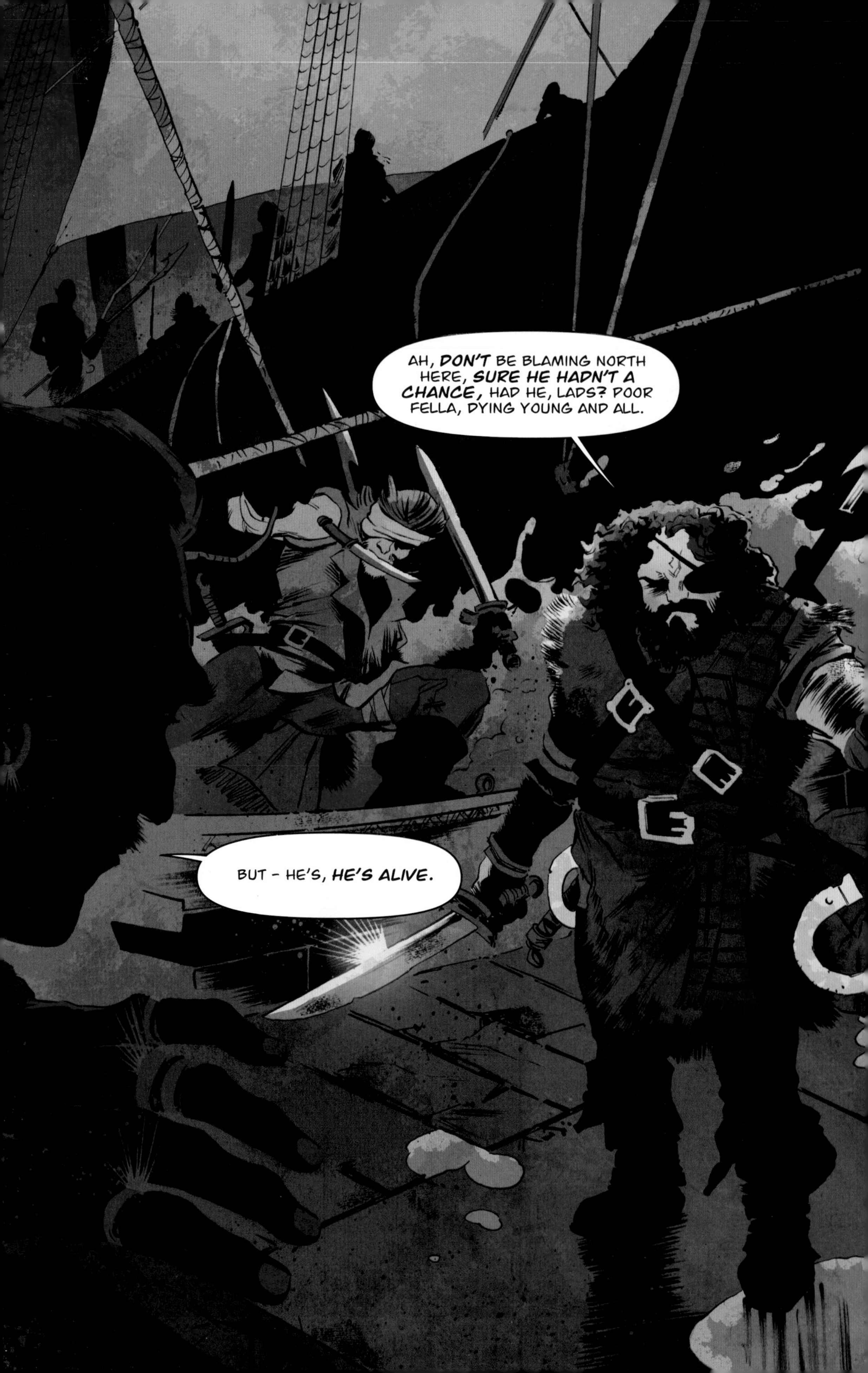
AH, **DON'T** BE BLAMING NORTH HERE, **SURE HE HADN'T A CHANCE,** HAD HE, LADS? POOR FELLA, DYING YOUNG AND ALL.
BUT - HE'S, **HE'S ALIVE.**

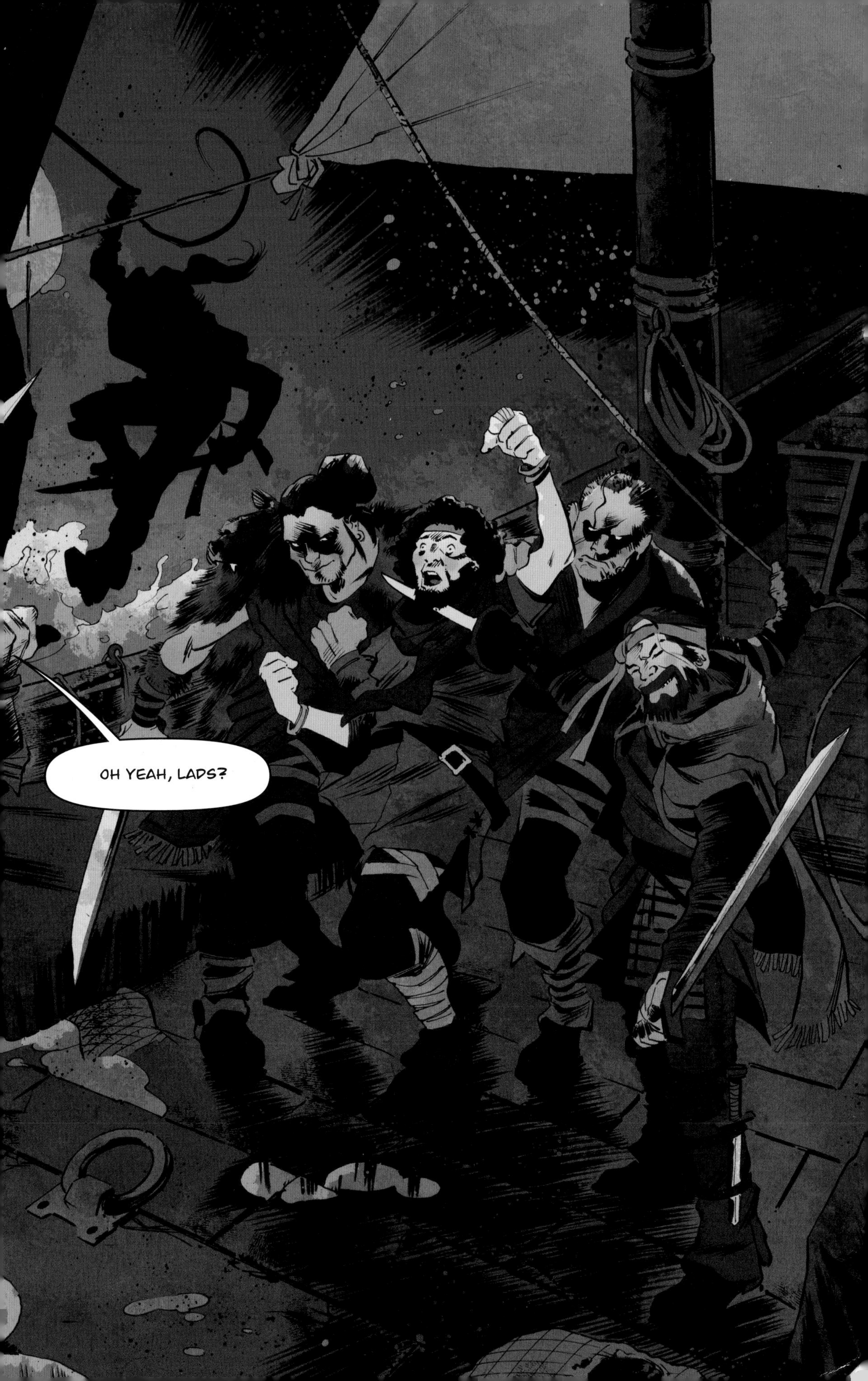
OH YEAH, LADS?

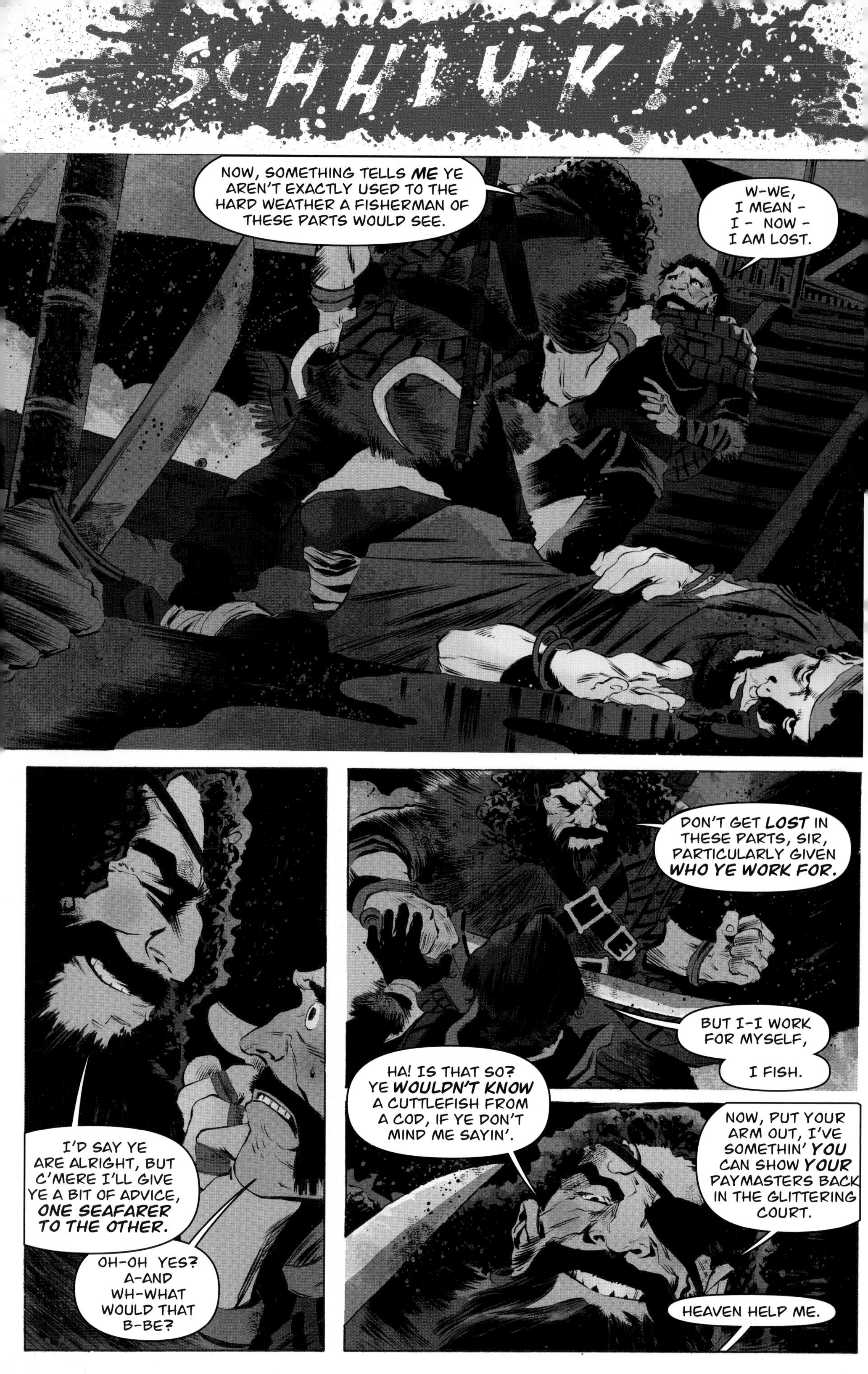
SCHHLUK!
NOW, SOMETHING TELLS ME YE AREN'T EXACTLY USED TO THE HARD WEATHER A FISHERMAN OF THESE PARTS WOULD SEE.
W-WE, I MEAN - I - NOW - I AM LOST.
I'D SAY YE ARE ALRIGHT, BUT C'MERE I'LL GIVE YE A BIT OF ADVICE, ONE SEAFARER TO THE OTHER.
OH-OH YES? A-AND WH-WHAT WOULD THAT B-BE?
DON'T GET LOST IN THESE PARTS, SIR, PARTICULARLY GIVEN WHO YE WORK FOR.
BUT I-I WORK FOR MYSELF,
I FISH.
HA! IS THAT SO? YE WOULDN'T KNOW A CUTTLEFISH FROM A COD, IF YE DON'T MIND ME SAYIN'.
NOW, PUT YOUR ARM OUT, I'VE SOMETHIN' YOU CAN SHOW YOUR PAYMASTERS BACK IN THE GLITTERING COURT.
HEAVEN HELP ME.

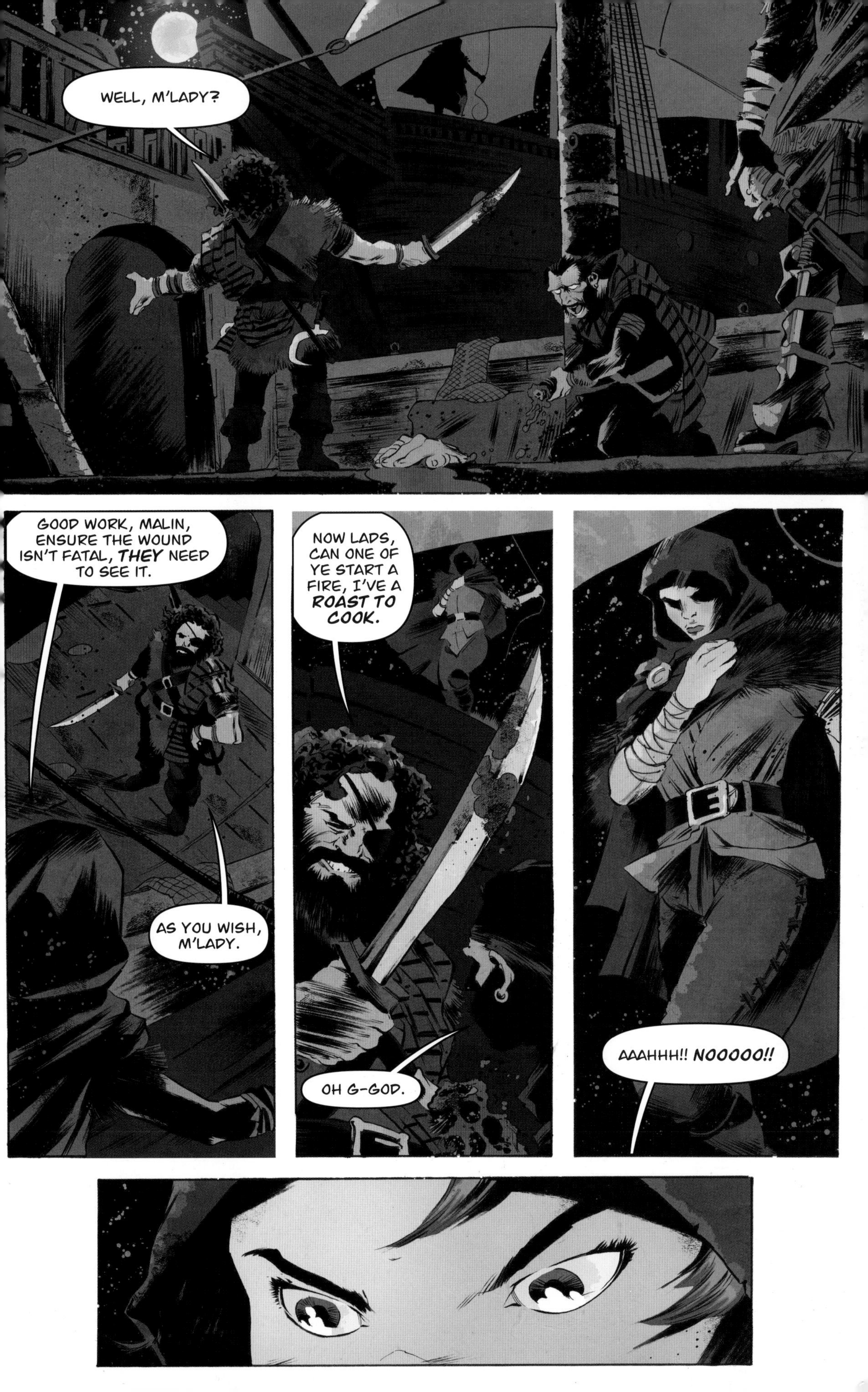
WELL, M'LADY?
GOOD WORK, MALIN, ENSURE THE WOUND ISN'T FATAL, *THEY* NEED TO SEE IT.
AS YOU WISH, M'LADY.
NOW LADS, CAN ONE OF YE START A FIRE, I'VE A ***ROAST TO COOK.***
OH G-GOD.
AAAHHH!! ***NOOOOO!!***

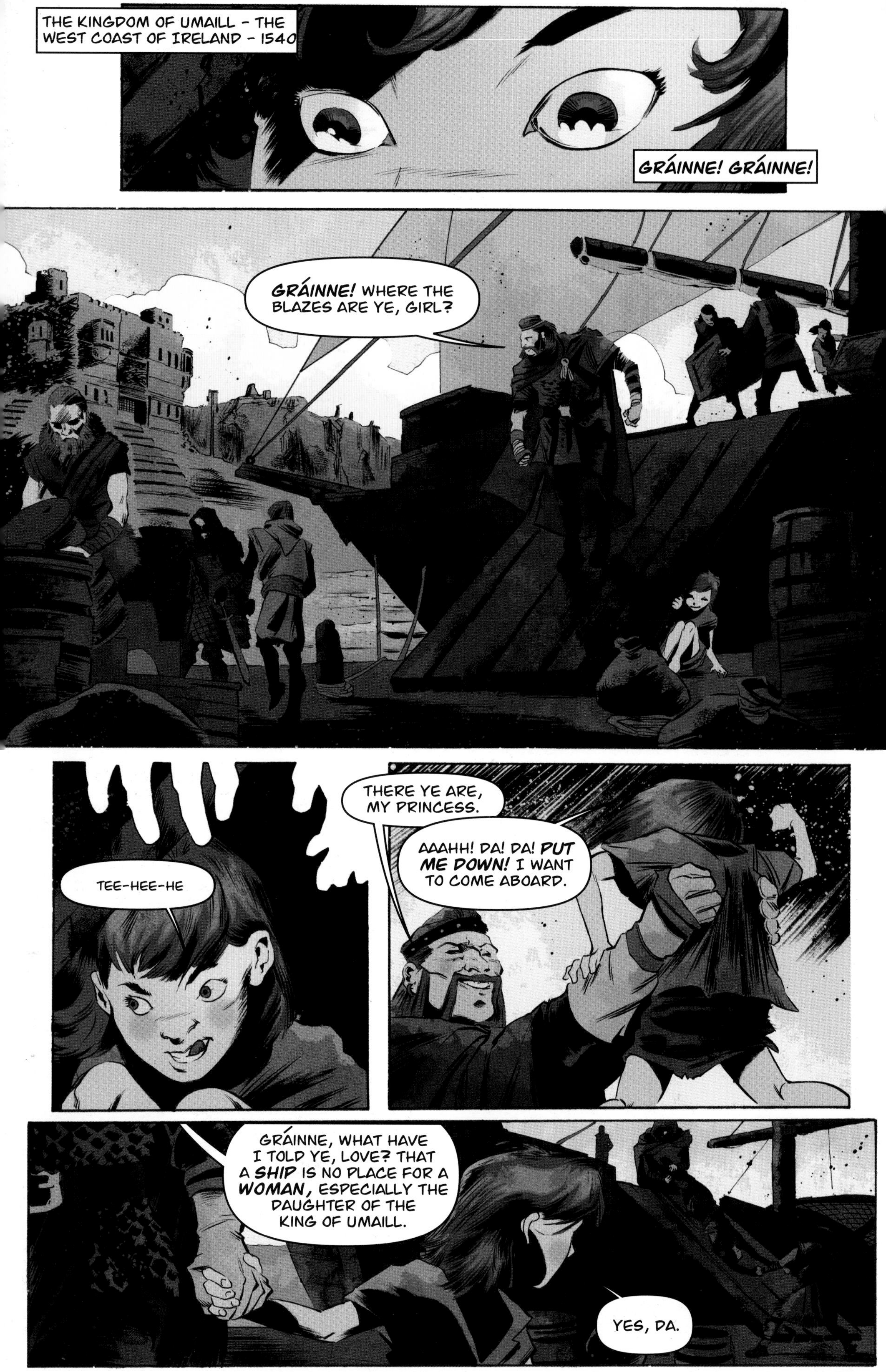
THE KINGDOM OF UMAILL – THE WEST COAST OF IRELAND – 1540
GRÁINNE! GRÁINNE!
GRÁINNE! WHERE THE BLAZES ARE YE, GIRL?
TEE-HEE-HE
THERE YE ARE, MY PRINCESS.
AAAHH! DA! DA! PUT ME DOWN! I WANT TO COME ABOARD.
GRÁINNE, WHAT HAVE I TOLD YE, LOVE? THAT A SHIP IS NO PLACE FOR A WOMAN, ESPECIALLY THE DAUGHTER OF THE KING OF UMAILL.
YES, DA.

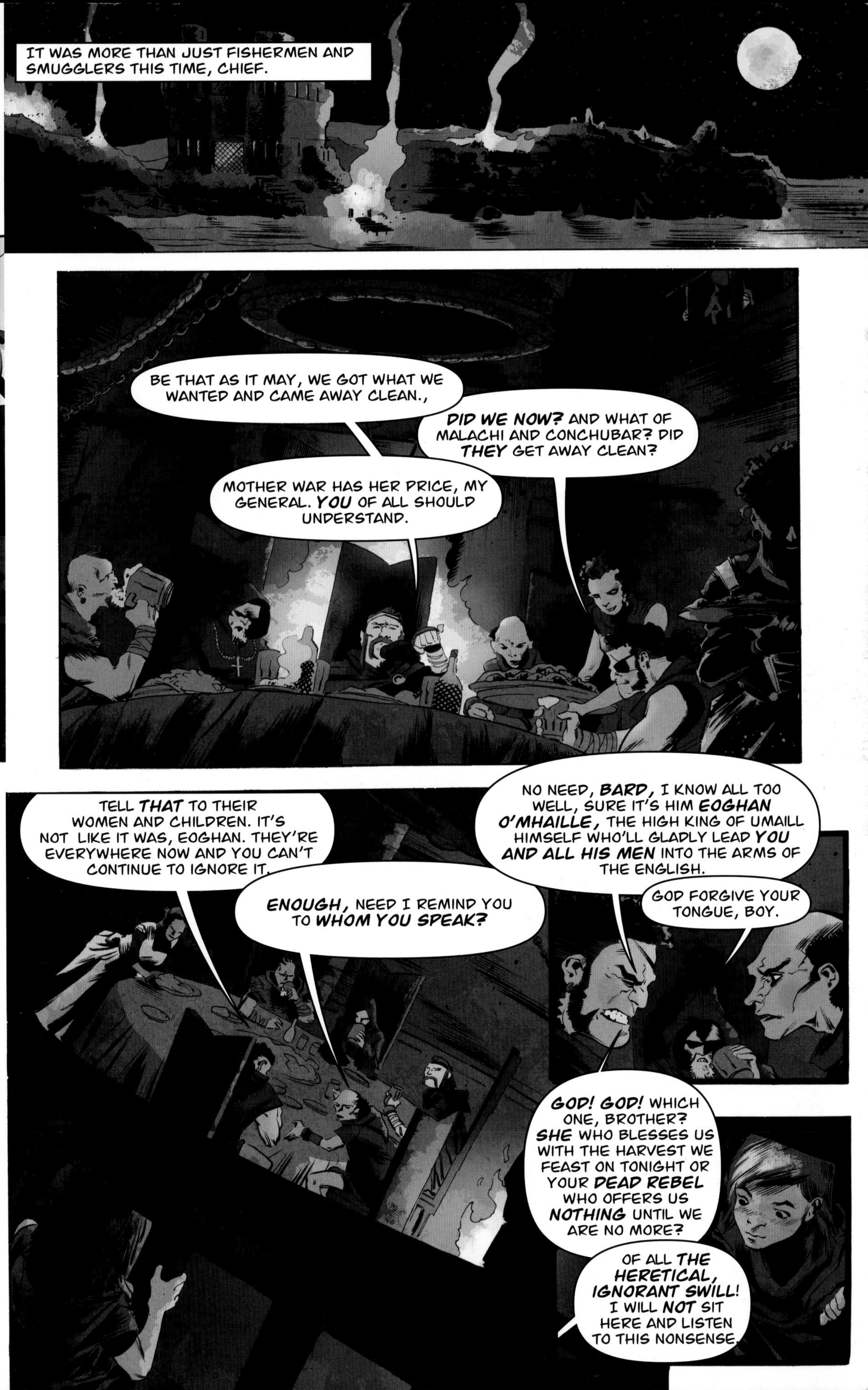
IT WAS MORE THAN JUST FISHERMEN AND SMUGGLERS THIS TIME, CHIEF.
BE THAT AS IT MAY, WE GOT WHAT WE WANTED AND CAME AWAY CLEAN.,
DID WE NOW? AND WHAT OF MALACHI AND CONCHUBAR? DID THEY GET AWAY CLEAN?
MOTHER WAR HAS HER PRICE, MY GENERAL. YOU OF ALL SHOULD UNDERSTAND.
TELL THAT TO THEIR WOMEN AND CHILDREN. IT'S NOT LIKE IT WAS, EOGHAN. THEY'RE EVERYWHERE NOW AND YOU CAN'T CONTINUE TO IGNORE IT.
ENOUGH, NEED I REMIND YOU TO WHOM YOU SPEAK?
NO NEED, BARD, I KNOW ALL TOO WELL, SURE IT'S HIM EOGHAN O'MHAILLE, THE HIGH KING OF UMAILL HIMSELF WHO'LL GLADLY LEAD YOU AND ALL HIS MEN INTO THE ARMS OF THE ENGLISH.
GOD FORGIVE YOUR TONGUE, BOY.
GOD! GOD! WHICH ONE, BROTHER? SHE WHO BLESSES US WITH THE HARVEST WE FEAST ON TONIGHT OR YOUR DEAD REBEL WHO OFFERS US NOTHING UNTIL WE ARE NO MORE?
OF ALL THE HERETICAL, IGNORANT SWILL! I WILL NOT SIT HERE AND LISTEN TO THIS NONSENSE.

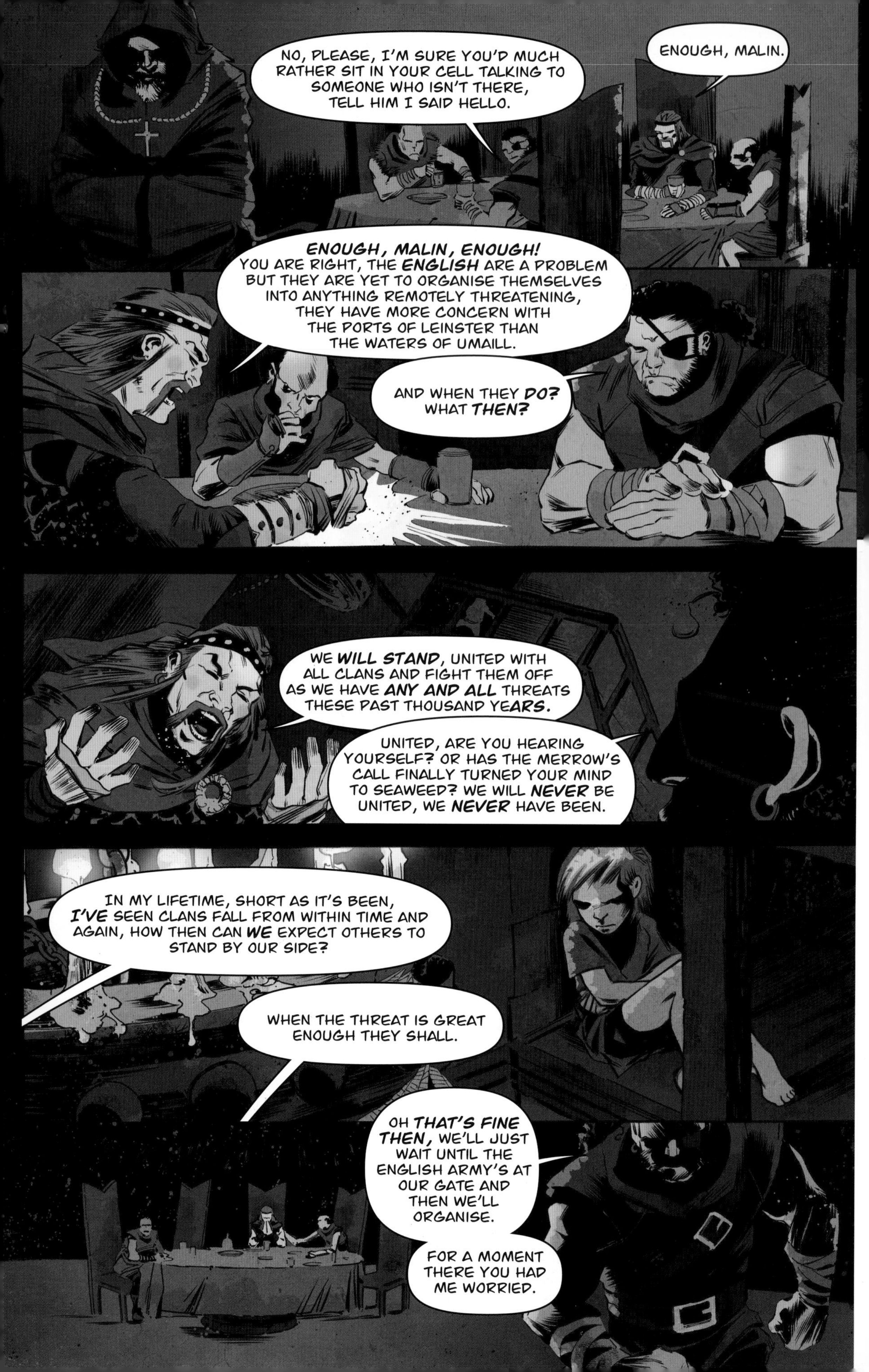

NO, PLEASE, I'M SURE YOU'D MUCH RATHER SIT IN YOUR CELL TALKING TO SOMEONE WHO ISN'T THERE, TELL HIM I SAID HELLO.
ENOUGH, MALIN.
ENOUGH, MALIN, ENOUGH! YOU ARE RIGHT, THE ENGLISH ARE A PROBLEM BUT THEY ARE YET TO ORGANISE THEMSELVES INTO ANYTHING REMOTELY THREATENING, THEY HAVE MORE CONCERN WITH THE PORTS OF LEINSTER THAN THE WATERS OF UMAILL.
AND WHEN THEY DO? WHAT THEN?
WE WILL STAND, UNITED WITH ALL CLANS AND FIGHT THEM OFF AS WE HAVE ANY AND ALL THREATS THESE PAST THOUSAND YEARS.
UNITED, ARE YOU HEARING YOURSELF? OR HAS THE MERROW'S CALL FINALLY TURNED YOUR MIND TO SEAWEED? WE WILL NEVER BE UNITED, WE NEVER HAVE BEEN.
IN MY LIFETIME, SHORT AS IT'S BEEN, I'VE SEEN CLANS FALL FROM WITHIN TIME AND AGAIN, HOW THEN CAN WE EXPECT OTHERS TO STAND BY OUR SIDE?
WHEN THE THREAT IS GREAT ENOUGH THEY SHALL.
OH THAT'S FINE THEN, WE'LL JUST WAIT UNTIL THE ENGLISH ARMY'S AT OUR GATE AND THEN WE'LL ORGANISE.
FOR A MOMENT THERE YOU HAD ME WORRIED.

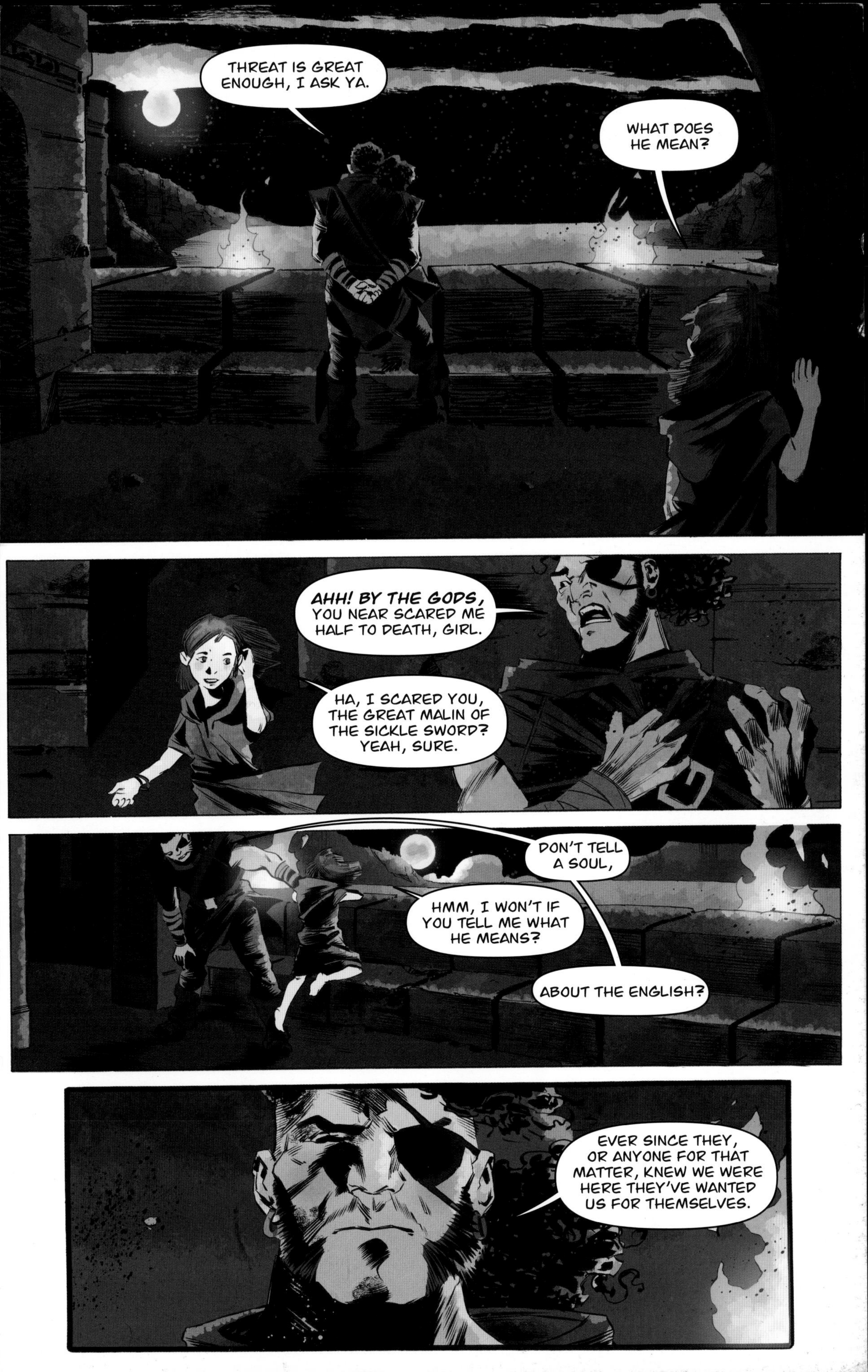
THREAT IS GREAT ENOUGH, I ASK YA.
WHAT DOES HE MEAN?
AHH! BY THE GODS, YOU NEAR SCARED ME HALF TO DEATH, GIRL.
HA, I SCARED YOU, THE GREAT MALIN OF THE SICKLE SWORD? YEAH, SURE.
DON'T TELL A SOUL,
HMM, I WON'T IF YOU TELL ME WHAT HE MEANS?
ABOUT THE ENGLISH?
EVER SINCE THEY, OR ANYONE FOR THAT MATTER, KNEW WE WERE HERE THEY'VE WANTED US FOR THEMSELVES.

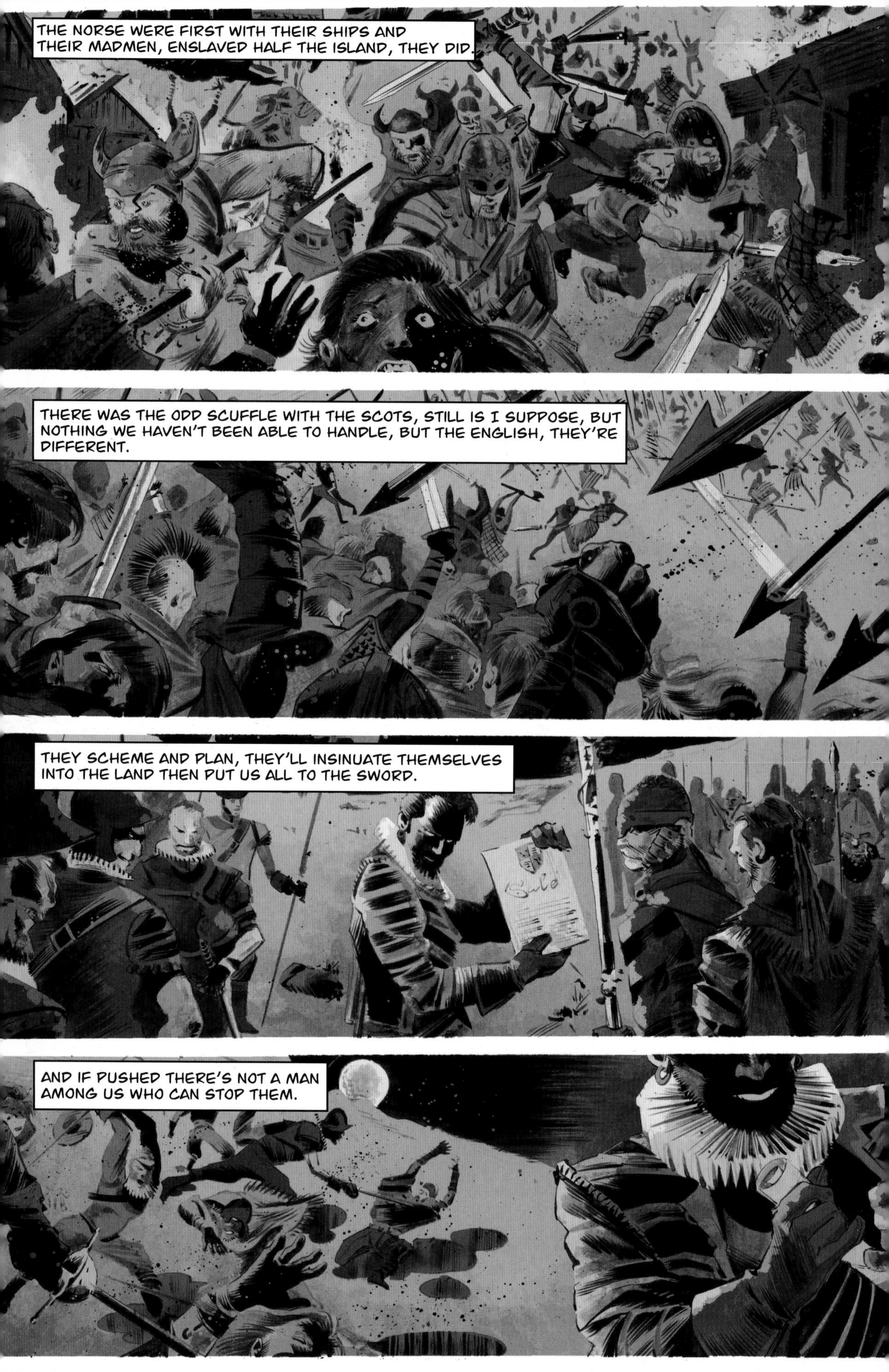
THE NORSE WERE FIRST WITH THEIR SHIPS AND THEIR MADMEN, ENSLAVED HALF THE ISLAND, THEY DID.
THERE WAS THE ODD SCUFFLE WITH THE SCOTS, STILL IS I SUPPOSE, BUT NOTHING WE HAVEN'T BEEN ABLE TO HANDLE, BUT THE ENGLISH, THEY'RE DIFFERENT.
THEY SCHEME AND PLAN, THEY'LL INSINUATE THEMSELVES INTO THE LAND THEN PUT US ALL TO THE SWORD.
AND IF PUSHED THERE'S NOT A MAN AMONG US WHO CAN STOP THEM.

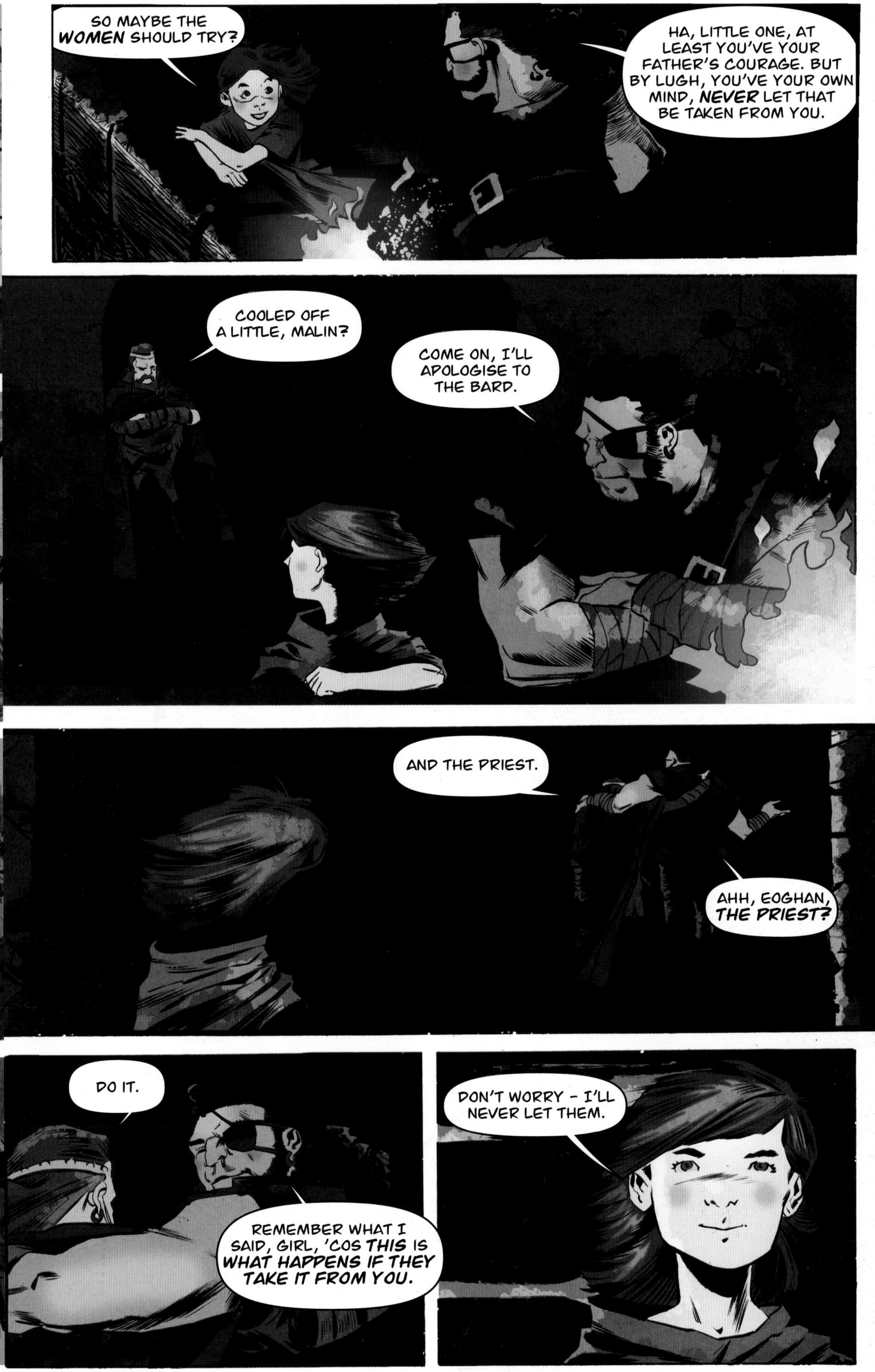
SO MAYBE THE **WOMEN** SHOULD TRY?
HA, LITTLE ONE, AT LEAST YOU'VE YOUR FATHER'S COURAGE. BUT BY LUGH, YOU'VE YOUR OWN MIND, ***NEVER*** LET THAT BE TAKEN FROM YOU.
COOLED OFF A LITTLE, MALIN?
COME ON, I'LL APOLOGISE TO THE BARD.
AND THE PRIEST.
AHH, EOGHAN, ***THE PRIEST?***
DO IT.
REMEMBER WHAT I SAID, GIRL, 'COS **THIS** IS ***WHAT HAPPENS IF THEY TAKE IT FROM YOU.***
DON'T WORRY – I'LL NEVER LET THEM.

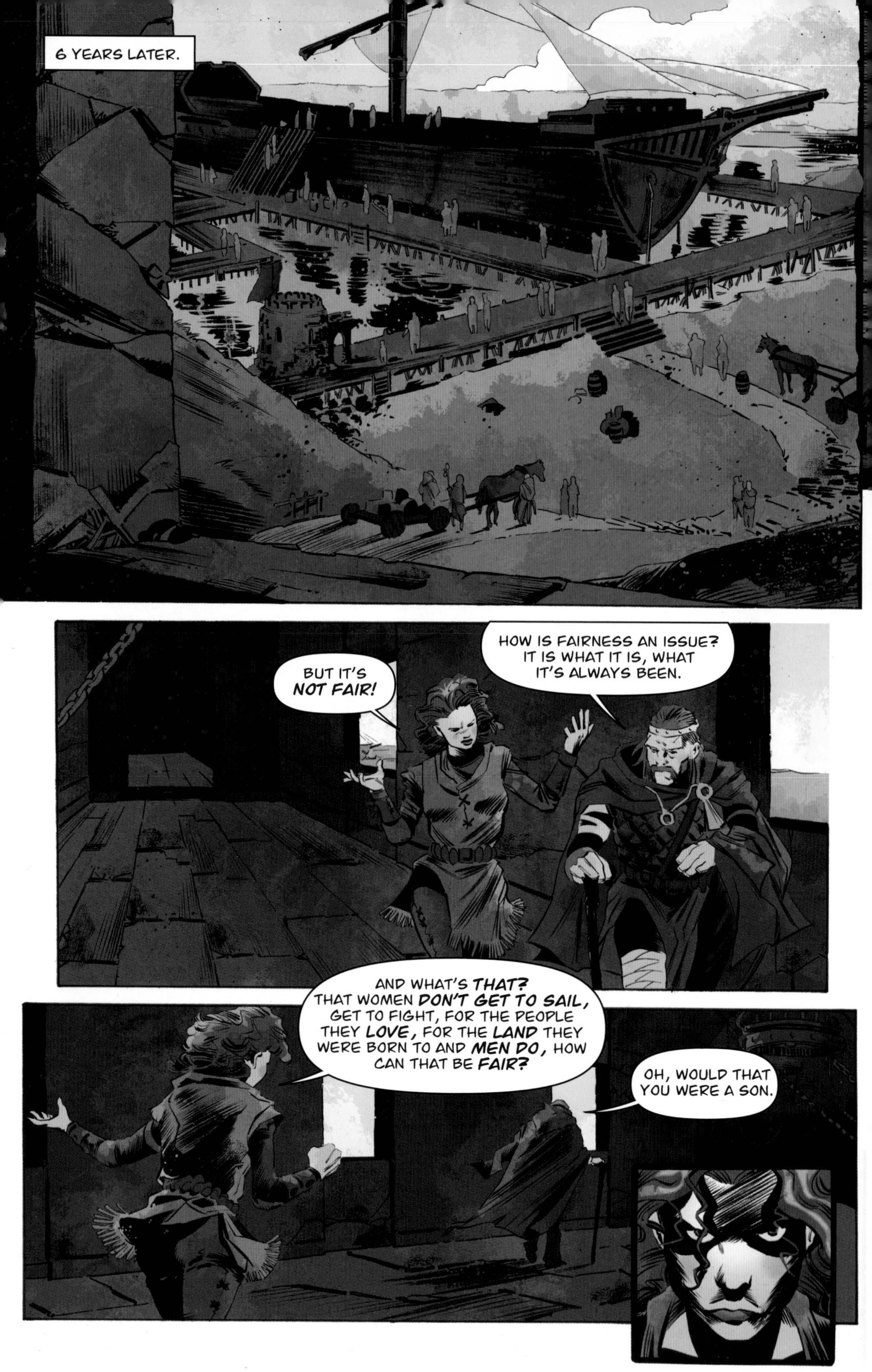
6 YEARS LATER.
BUT IT'S NOT FAIR!
HOW IS FAIRNESS AN ISSUE? IT IS WHAT IT IS, WHAT IT'S ALWAYS BEEN.
AND WHAT'S THAT? THAT WOMEN DON'T GET TO SAIL, GET TO FIGHT, FOR THE PEOPLE THEY LOVE, FOR THE LAND THEY WERE BORN TO AND MEN DO, HOW CAN THAT BE FAIR?
OH, WOULD THAT YOU WERE A SON.

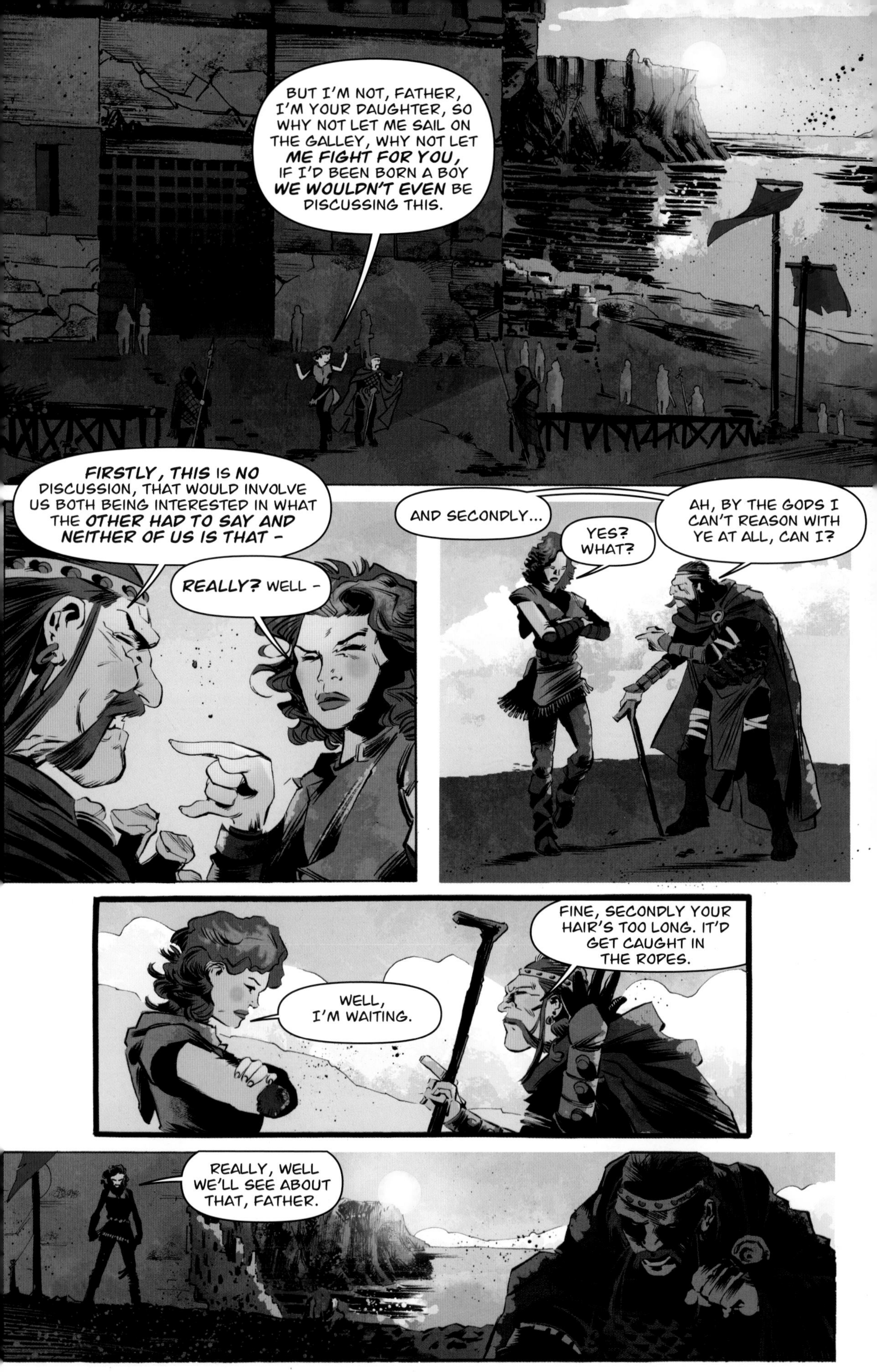
BUT I'M NOT, FATHER, I'M YOUR DAUGHTER, SO WHY NOT LET ME SAIL ON THE GALLEY, WHY NOT LET ME FIGHT FOR YOU, IF I'D BEEN BORN A BOY WE WOULDN'T EVEN BE DISCUSSING THIS.
FIRSTLY, THIS IS NO DISCUSSION, THAT WOULD INVOLVE US BOTH BEING INTERESTED IN WHAT THE OTHER HAD TO SAY AND NEITHER OF US IS THAT -
REALLY? WELL -
AND SECONDLY...
YES? WHAT?
AH, BY THE GODS I CAN'T REASON WITH YE AT ALL, CAN I?
WELL, I'M WAITING.
FINE, SECONDLY YOUR HAIR'S TOO LONG. IT'D GET CAUGHT IN THE ROPES.
REALLY, WELL WE'LL SEE ABOUT THAT, FATHER.

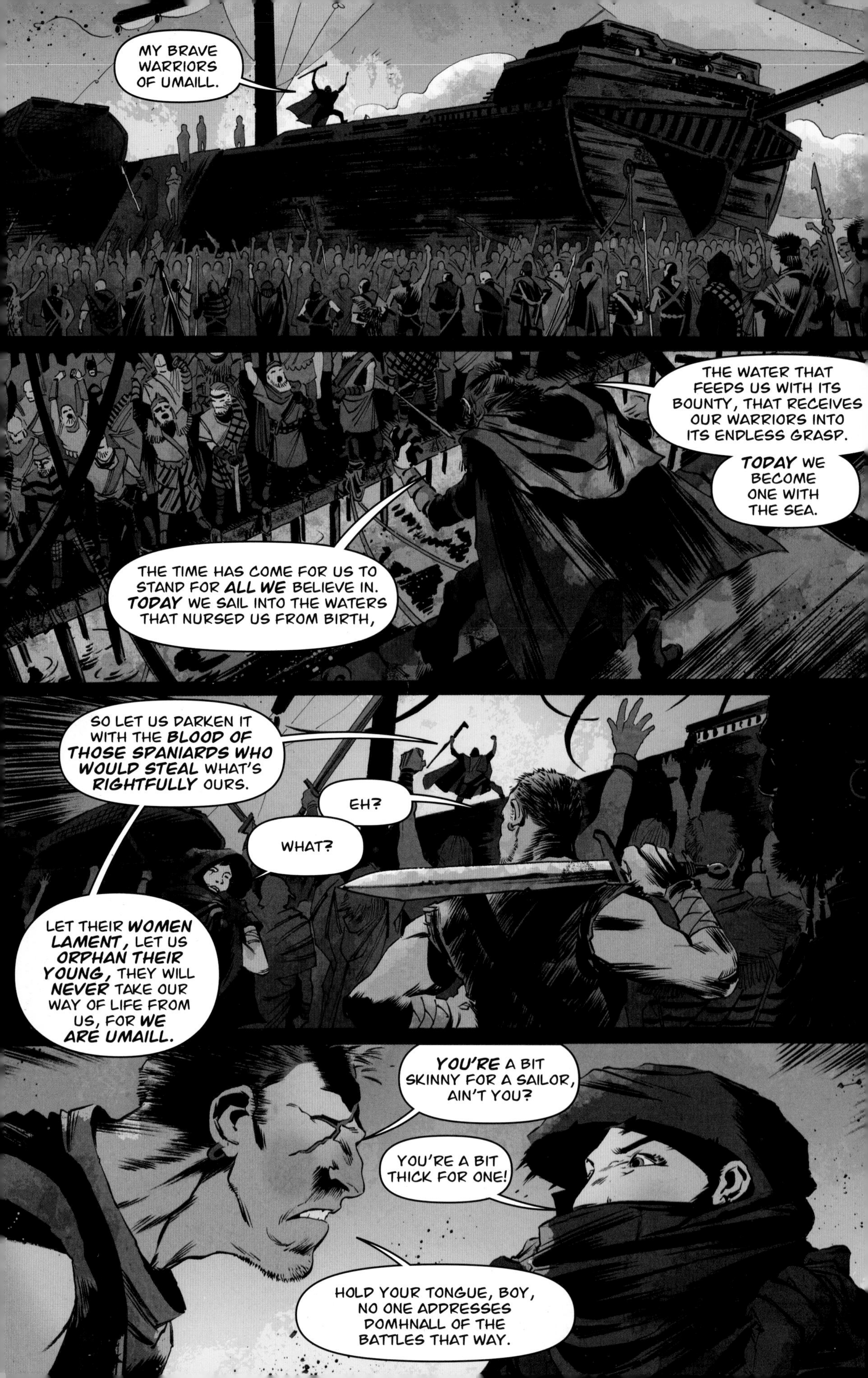
MY BRAVE WARRIORS OF UMAILL.
THE TIME HAS COME FOR US TO STAND FOR **ALL WE** BELIEVE IN. ***TODAY*** WE SAIL INTO THE WATERS THAT NURSED US FROM BIRTH,
THE WATER THAT FEEDS US WITH ITS BOUNTY, THAT RECEIVES OUR WARRIORS INTO ITS ENDLESS GRASP.
TODAY WE BECOME ONE WITH THE SEA.
SO LET US DARKEN IT WITH THE ***BLOOD OF THOSE SPANIARDS WHO WOULD STEAL*** WHAT'S ***RIGHTFULLY*** OURS.
EH?
WHAT?
LET THEIR ***WOMEN LAMENT***, LET US ***ORPHAN THEIR YOUNG***, THEY WILL ***NEVER*** TAKE OUR WAY OF LIFE FROM US, FOR ***WE ARE UMAILL.***
YOU'RE A BIT SKINNY FOR A SAILOR, AIN'T YOU?
YOU'RE A BIT THICK FOR ONE!
HOLD YOUR TONGUE, BOY, NO ONE ADDRESSES DOMHNALL OF THE BATTLES THAT WAY.

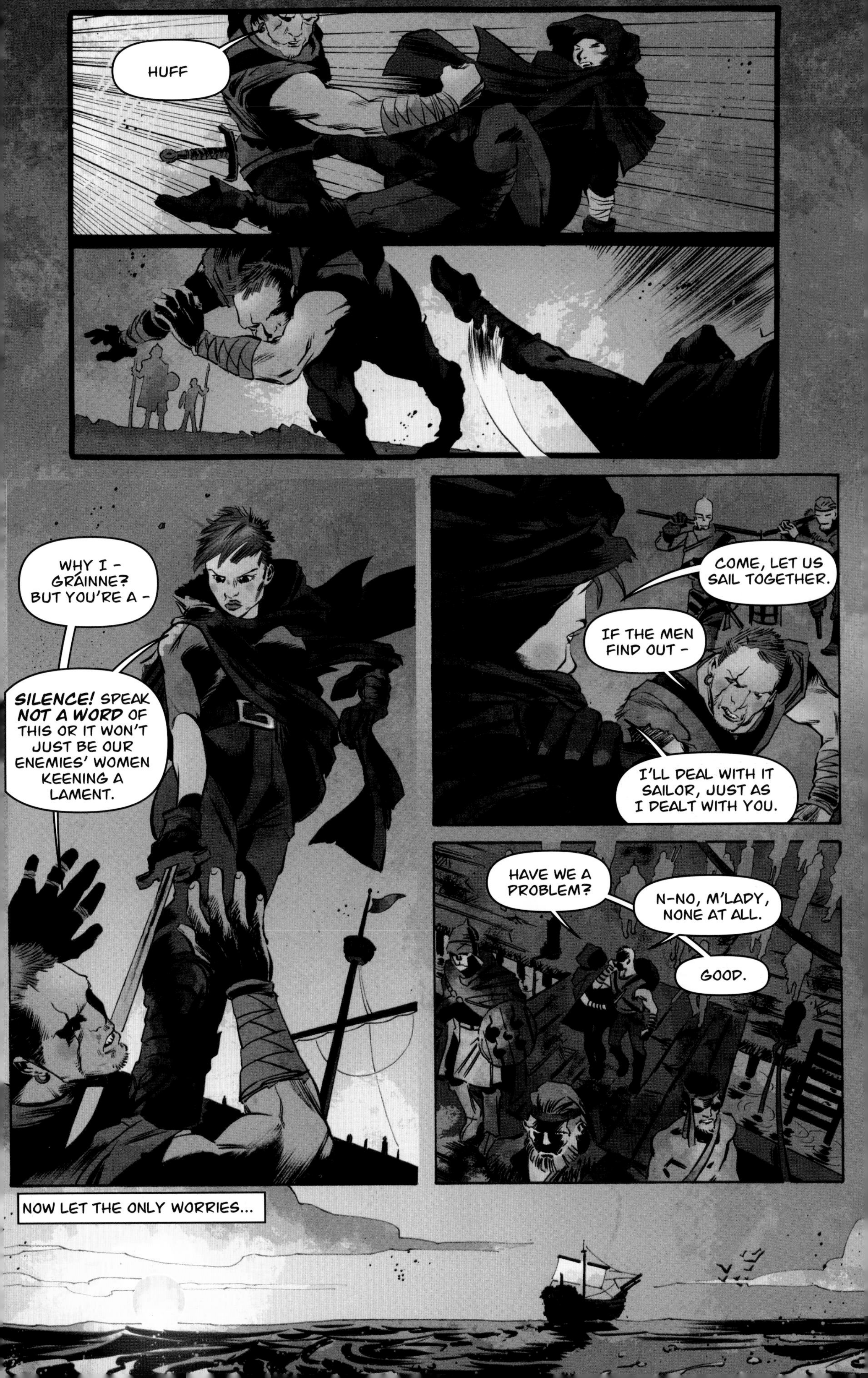
HUFF
WHY I - GRÁINNE? BUT YOU'RE A -
SILENCE! SPEAK NOT A WORD OF THIS OR IT WON'T JUST BE OUR ENEMIES' WOMEN KEENING A LAMENT.
COME, LET US SAIL TOGETHER.
IF THE MEN FIND OUT -
I'LL DEAL WITH IT SAILOR, JUST AS I DEALT WITH YOU.
HAVE WE A PROBLEM?
N-NO, M'LADY, NONE AT ALL.
GOOD.
NOW LET THE ONLY WORRIES...

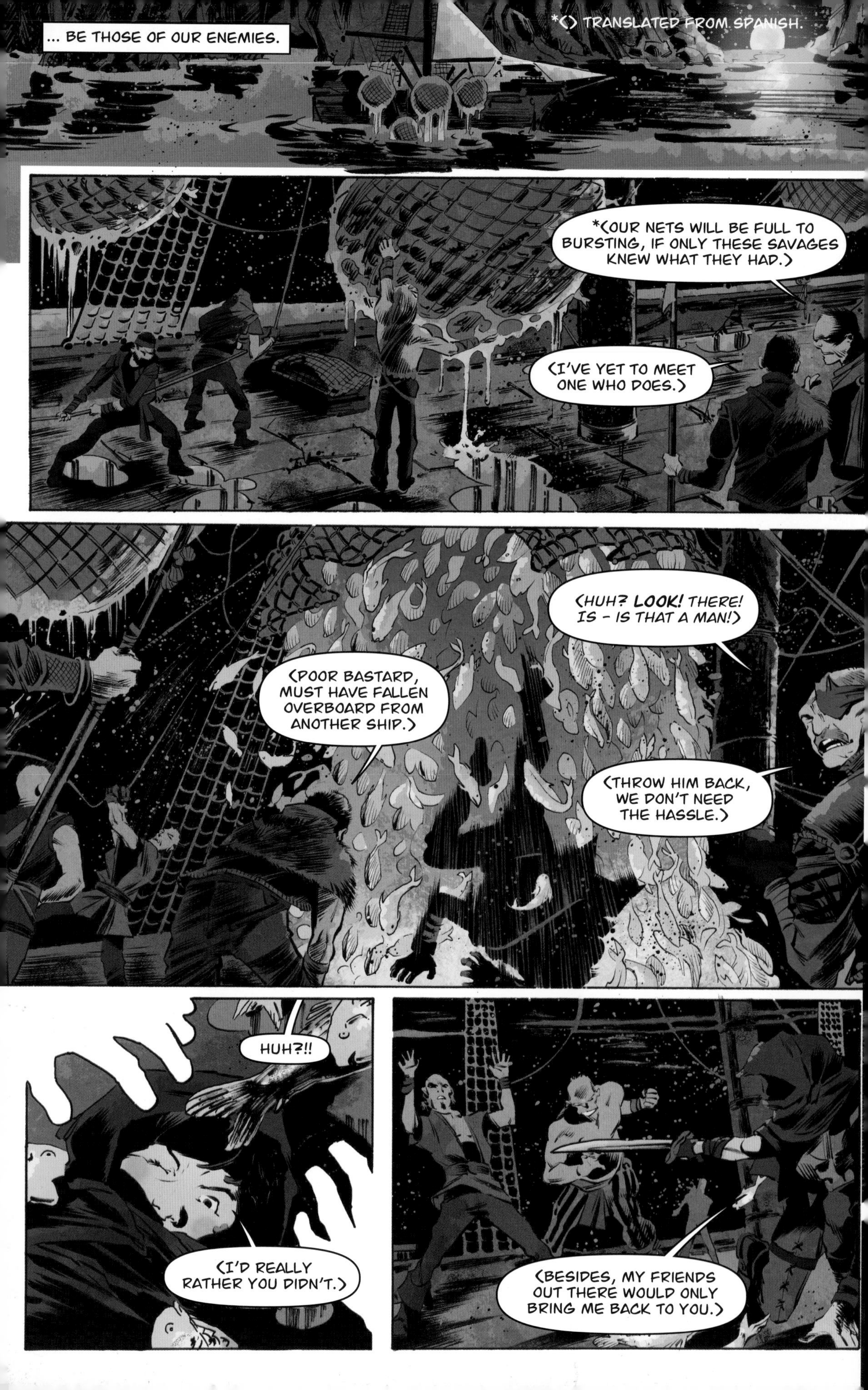
... BE THOSE OF OUR ENEMIES.
*⟨⟩ TRANSLATED FROM SPANISH.
*⟨OUR NETS WILL BE FULL TO BURSTING, IF ONLY THESE SAVAGES KNEW WHAT THEY HAD.⟩
⟨I'VE YET TO MEET ONE WHO DOES.⟩
⟨HUH? LOOK! THERE! IS - IS THAT A MAN!⟩
⟨POOR BASTARD, MUST HAVE FALLEN OVERBOARD FROM ANOTHER SHIP.⟩
⟨THROW HIM BACK, WE DON'T NEED THE HASSLE.⟩
HUH?!!
⟨I'D REALLY RATHER YOU DIDN'T.⟩
⟨BESIDES, MY FRIENDS OUT THERE WOULD ONLY BRING ME BACK TO YOU.⟩

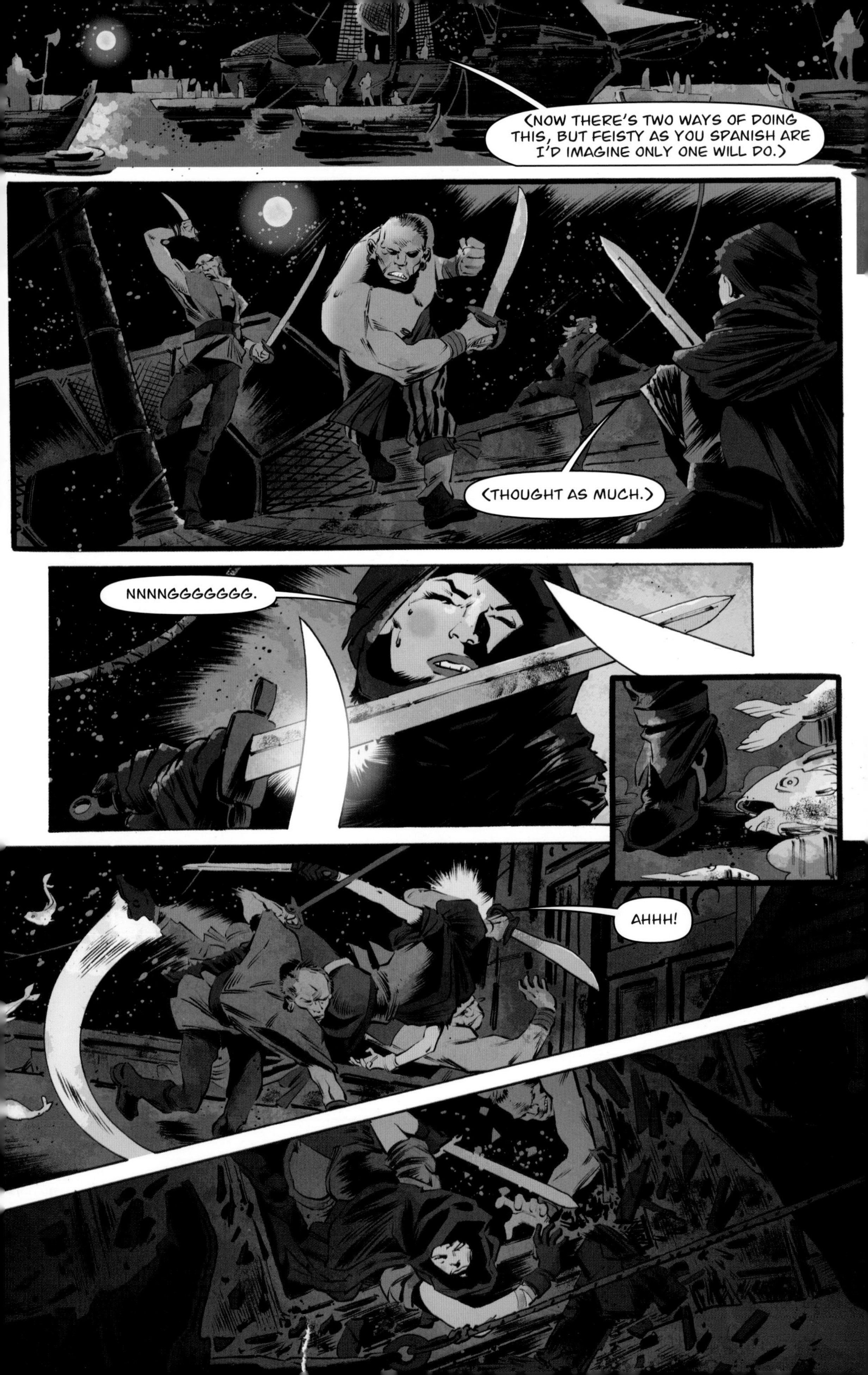
(NOW THERE'S TWO WAYS OF DOING THIS, BUT FEISTY AS YOU SPANISH ARE I'D IMAGINE ONLY ONE WILL DO.)
(THOUGHT AS MUCH.)
NNNNGGGGGGG.
AHHH!

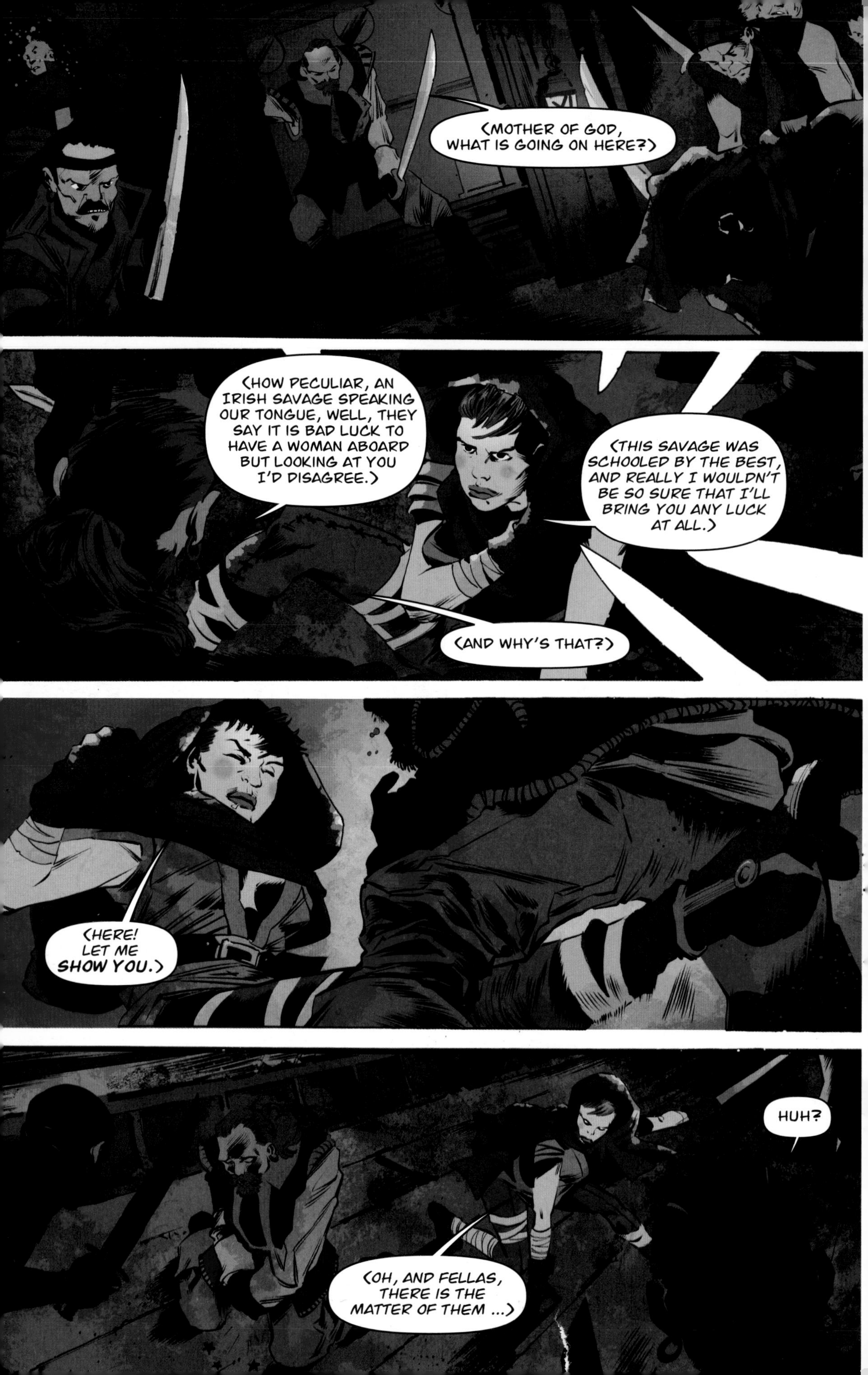

(MOTHER OF GOD, WHAT IS GOING ON HERE?)
(HOW PECULIAR, AN IRISH SAVAGE SPEAKING OUR TONGUE, WELL, THEY SAY IT IS BAD LUCK TO HAVE A WOMAN ABOARD BUT LOOKING AT YOU I'D DISAGREE.)
(THIS SAVAGE WAS SCHOOLED BY THE BEST, AND REALLY I WOULDN'T BE SO SURE THAT I'LL BRING YOU ANY LUCK AT ALL.)
(AND WHY'S THAT?)
(HERE! LET ME SHOW YOU.)
HUH?
(OH, AND FELLAS, THERE IS THE MATTER OF THEM ...)

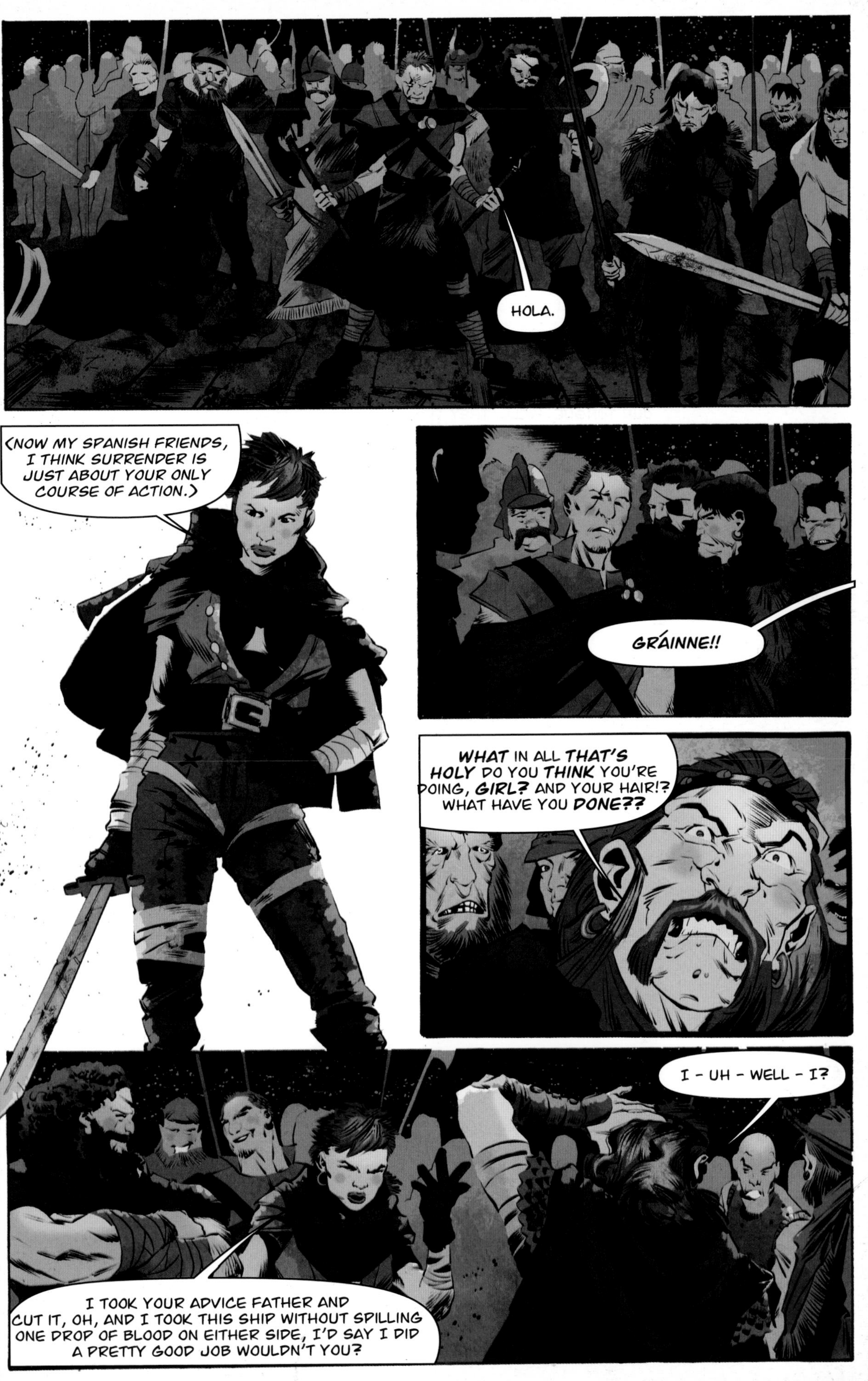
HOLA.
<NOW MY SPANISH FRIENDS, I THINK SURRENDER IS JUST ABOUT YOUR ONLY COURSE OF ACTION.>
GRÁINNE!!
WHAT IN ALL THAT'S HOLY DO YOU THINK YOU'RE DOING, GIRL? AND YOUR HAIR!? WHAT HAVE YOU DONE??
I - UH - WELL - I?
I TOOK YOUR ADVICE FATHER AND CUT IT, OH, AND I TOOK THIS SHIP WITHOUT SPILLING ONE DROP OF BLOOD ON EITHER SIDE, I'D SAY I DID A PRETTY GOOD JOB WOULDN'T YOU?

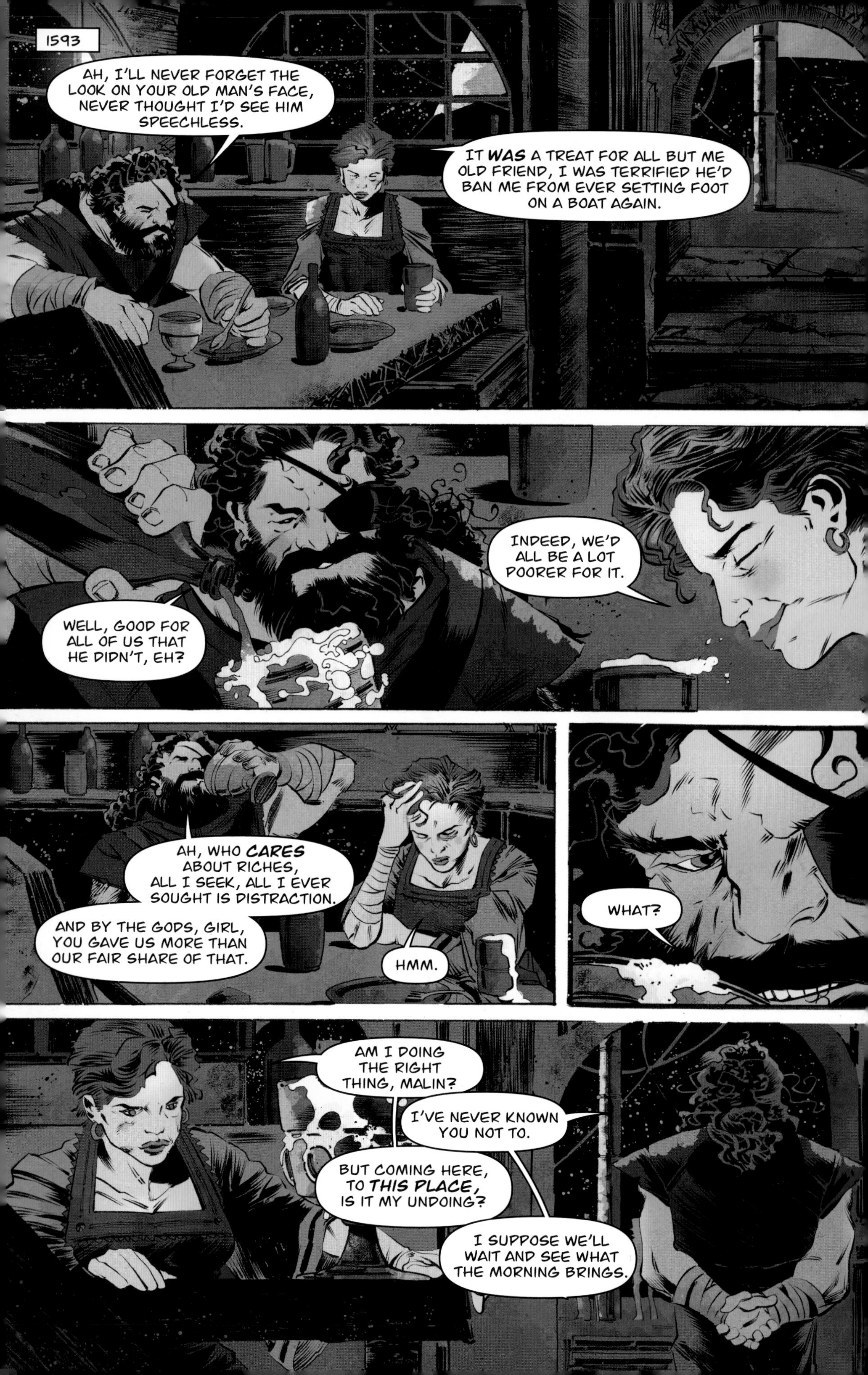
1593
AH, I'LL NEVER FORGET THE LOOK ON YOUR OLD MAN'S FACE, NEVER THOUGHT I'D SEE HIM SPEECHLESS.
IT **WAS** A TREAT FOR ALL BUT ME OLD FRIEND, I WAS TERRIFIED HE'D BAN ME FROM EVER SETTING FOOT ON A BOAT AGAIN.
WELL, GOOD FOR ALL OF US THAT HE DIDN'T, EH?
INDEED, WE'D ALL BE A LOT POORER FOR IT.
AH, WHO **CARES** ABOUT RICHES, ALL I SEEK, ALL I EVER SOUGHT IS DISTRACTION.
AND BY THE GODS, GIRL, YOU GAVE US MORE THAN OUR FAIR SHARE OF THAT.
HMM.
WHAT?
AM I DOING THE RIGHT THING, MALIN?
I'VE NEVER KNOWN YOU NOT TO.
BUT COMING HERE, TO **THIS PLACE,** IS IT MY UNDOING?
I SUPPOSE WE'LL WAIT AND SEE WHAT THE MORNING BRINGS.

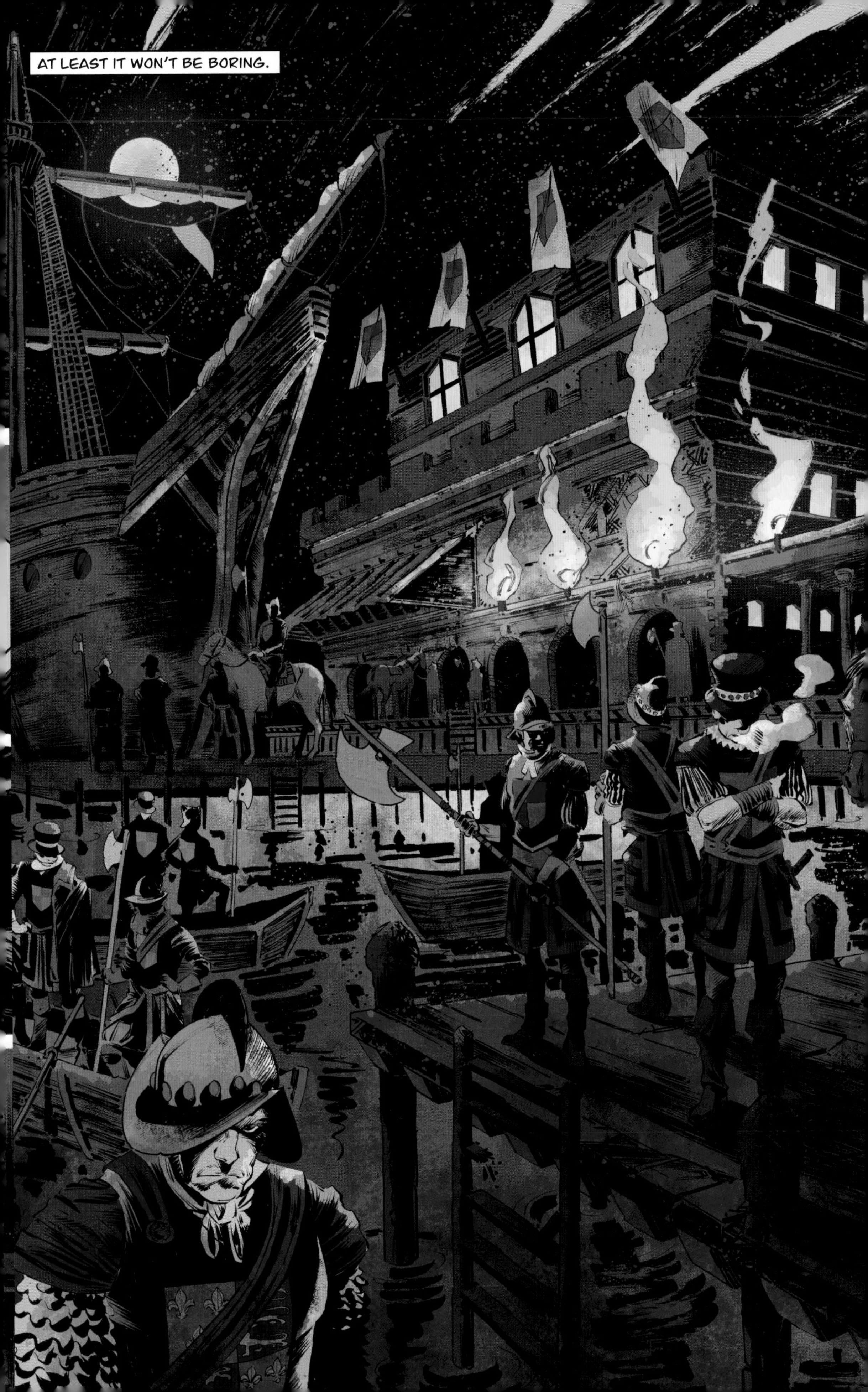
AT LEAST IT WON'T BE BORING.

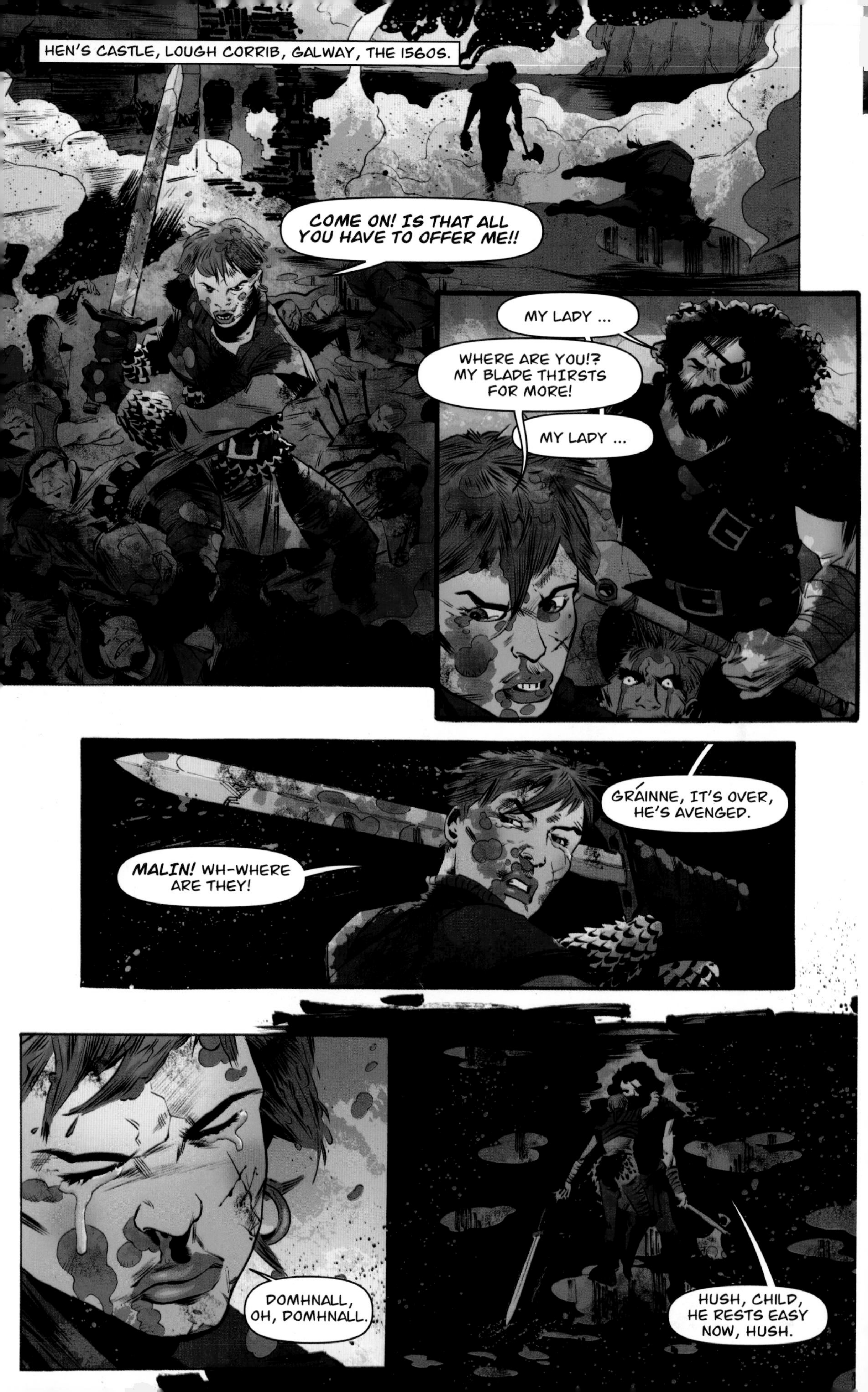
HEN'S CASTLE, LOUGH CORRIB, GALWAY, THE 1560S.
COME ON! IS THAT ALL YOU HAVE TO OFFER ME!!
MY LADY ...
WHERE ARE YOU!? MY BLADE THIRSTS FOR MORE!
MY LADY ...
GRÁINNE, IT'S OVER, HE'S AVENGED.
MALIN! WH-WHERE ARE THEY!
DOMHNALL, OH, DOMHNALL.
HUSH, CHILD, HE RESTS EASY NOW, HUSH.

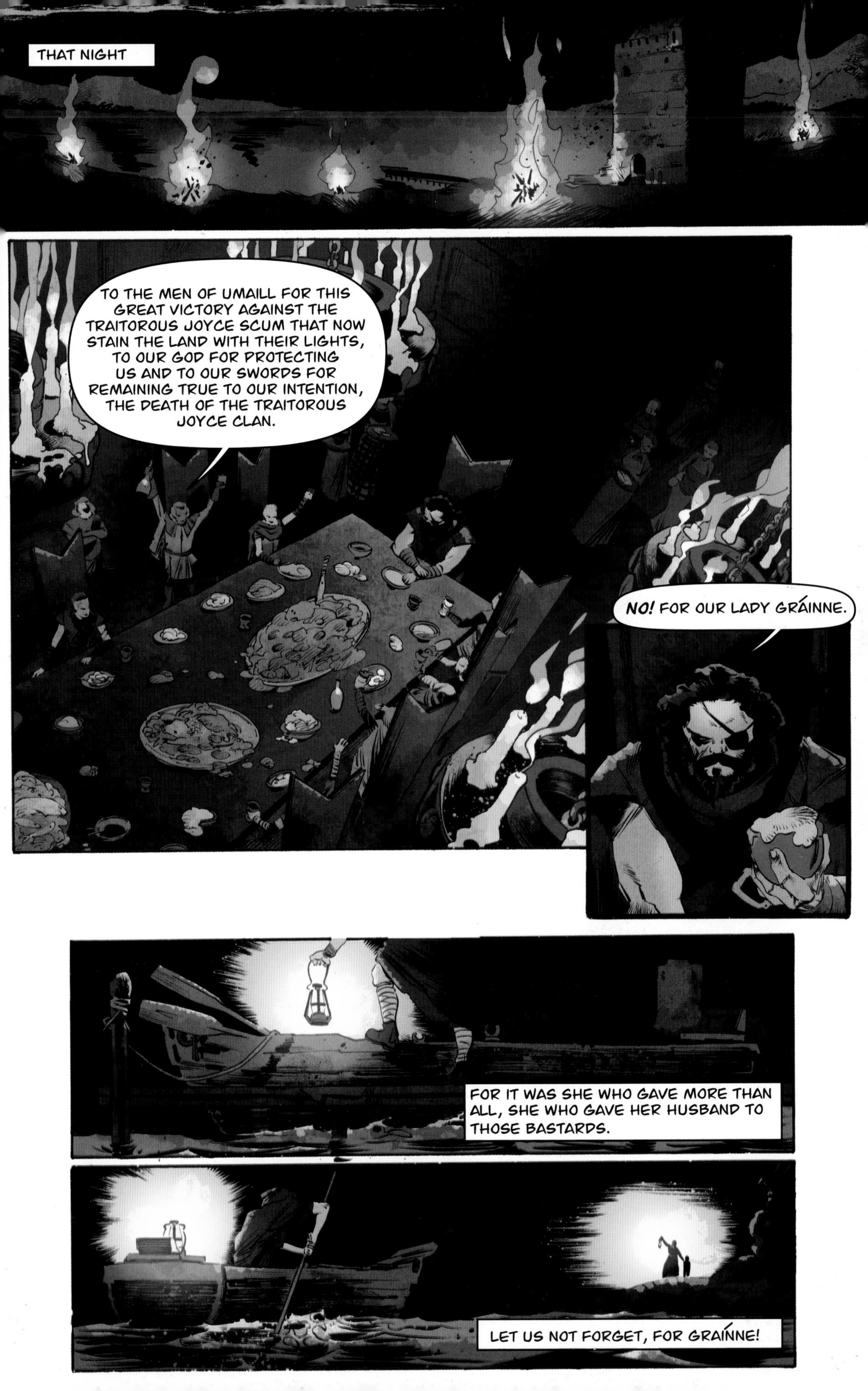
THAT NIGHT
TO THE MEN OF UMAILL FOR THIS GREAT VICTORY AGAINST THE TRAITOROUS JOYCE SCUM THAT NOW STAIN THE LAND WITH THEIR LIGHTS, TO OUR GOD FOR PROTECTING US AND TO OUR SWORDS FOR REMAINING TRUE TO OUR INTENTION, THE DEATH OF THE TRAITOROUS JOYCE CLAN.
NO! FOR OUR LADY GRÁINNE.
FOR IT WAS SHE WHO GAVE MORE THAN ALL, SHE WHO GAVE HER HUSBAND TO THOSE BASTARDS.
LET US NOT FORGET, FOR GRÁINNE!

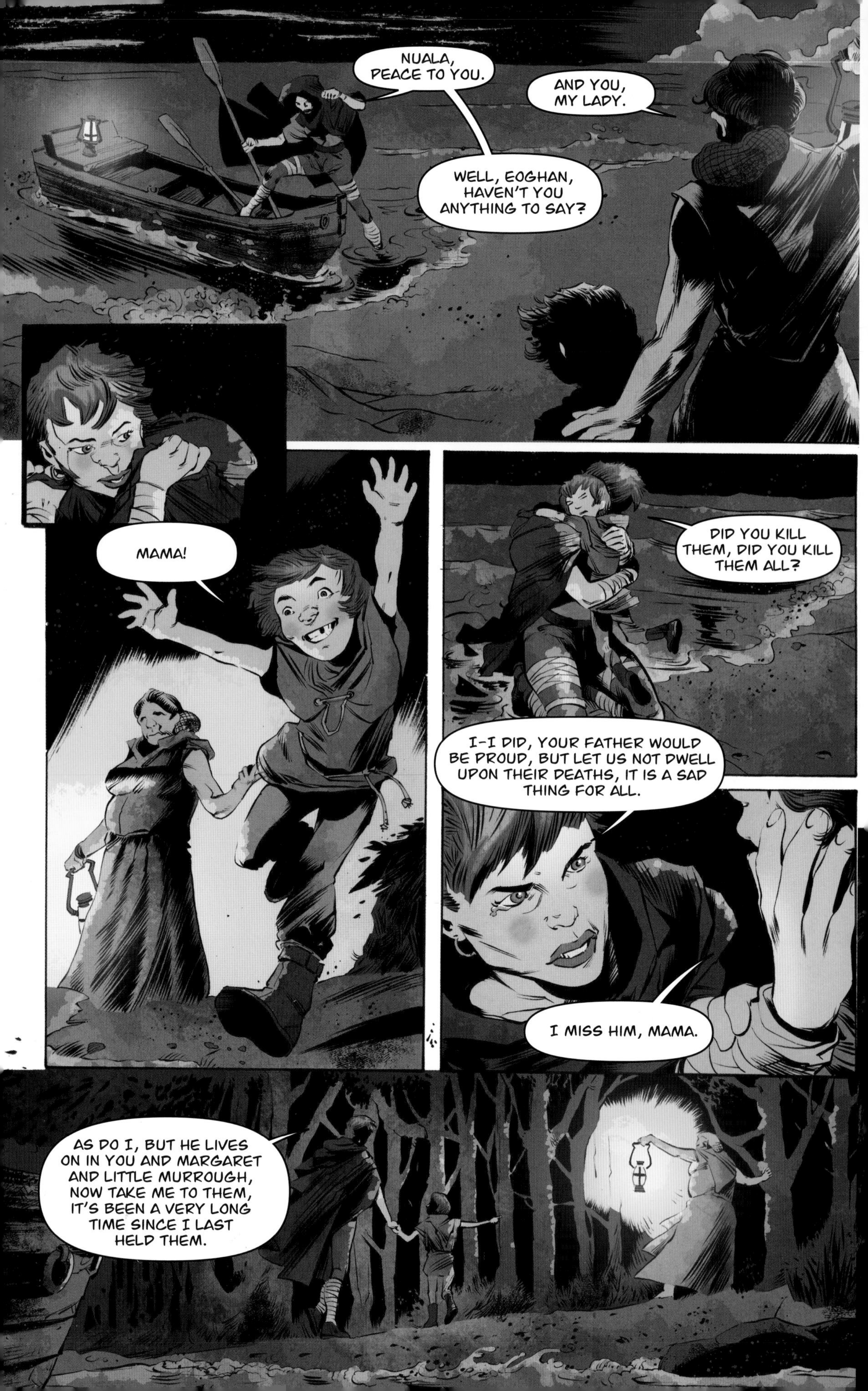
NUALA, PEACE TO YOU.
AND YOU, MY LADY.
WELL, EOGHAN, HAVEN'T YOU ANYTHING TO SAY?
MAMA!
DID YOU KILL THEM, DID YOU KILL THEM ALL?
I-I DID, YOUR FATHER WOULD BE PROUD, BUT LET US NOT DWELL UPON THEIR DEATHS, IT IS A SAD THING FOR ALL.
I MISS HIM, MAMA.
AS DO I, BUT HE LIVES ON IN YOU AND MARGARET AND LITTLE MURROUGH, NOW TAKE ME TO THEM, IT'S BEEN A VERY LONG TIME SINCE I LAST HELD THEM.

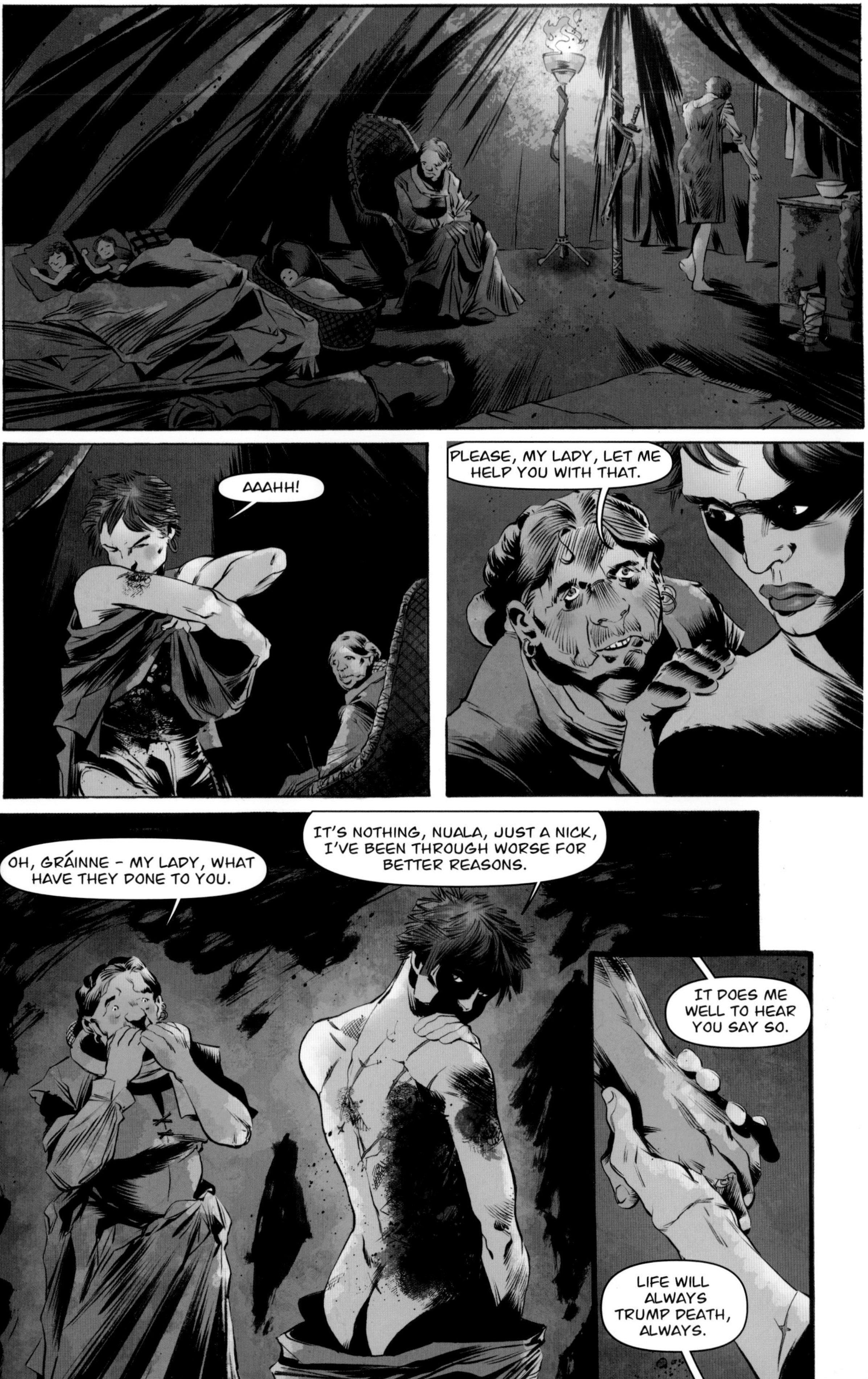
AAAHH!
PLEASE, MY LADY, LET ME HELP YOU WITH THAT.
OH, GRÁINNE - MY LADY, WHAT HAVE THEY DONE TO YOU.
IT'S NOTHING, NUALA, JUST A NICK, I'VE BEEN THROUGH WORSE FOR BETTER REASONS.
IT DOES ME WELL TO HEAR YOU SAY SO.
LIFE WILL ALWAYS TRUMP DEATH, ALWAYS.

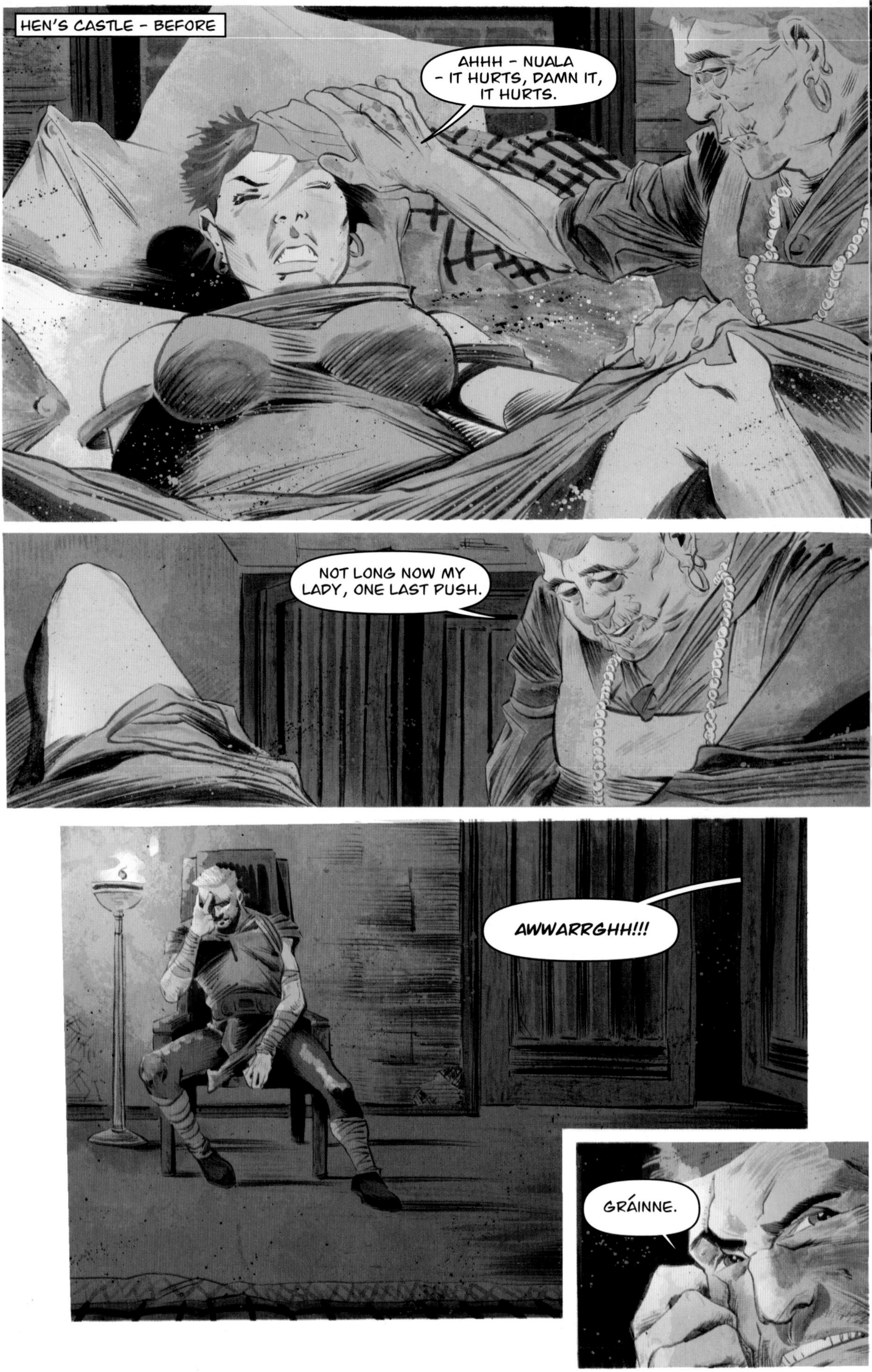
HEN'S CASTLE - BEFORE
AHHH - NUALA - IT HURTS, DAMN IT, IT HURTS.
NOT LONG NOW MY LADY, ONE LAST PUSH.
AWWARRGHH!!!
GRÁINNE.

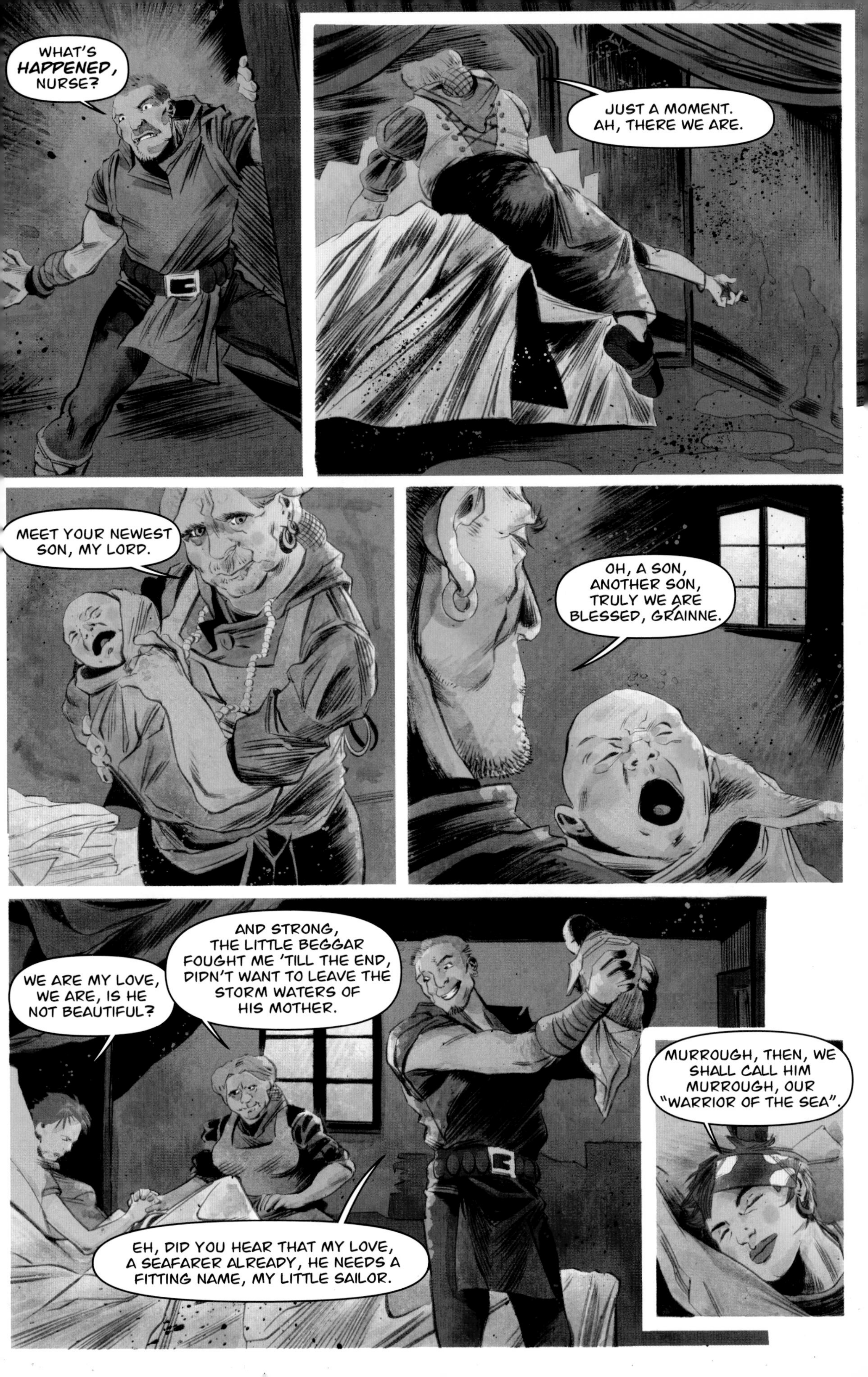
WHAT'S HAPPENED, NURSE?
JUST A MOMENT. AH, THERE WE ARE.
MEET YOUR NEWEST SON, MY LORD.
OH, A SON, ANOTHER SON, TRULY WE ARE BLESSED, GRAINNE.
WE ARE MY LOVE, WE ARE, IS HE NOT BEAUTIFUL?
AND STRONG, THE LITTLE BEGGAR FOUGHT ME 'TILL THE END, DIDN'T WANT TO LEAVE THE STORM WATERS OF HIS MOTHER.
EH, DID YOU HEAR THAT MY LOVE, A SEAFARER ALREADY, HE NEEDS A FITTING NAME, MY LITTLE SAILOR.
MURROUGH, THEN, WE SHALL CALL HIM MURROUGH, OUR "WARRIOR OF THE SEA".

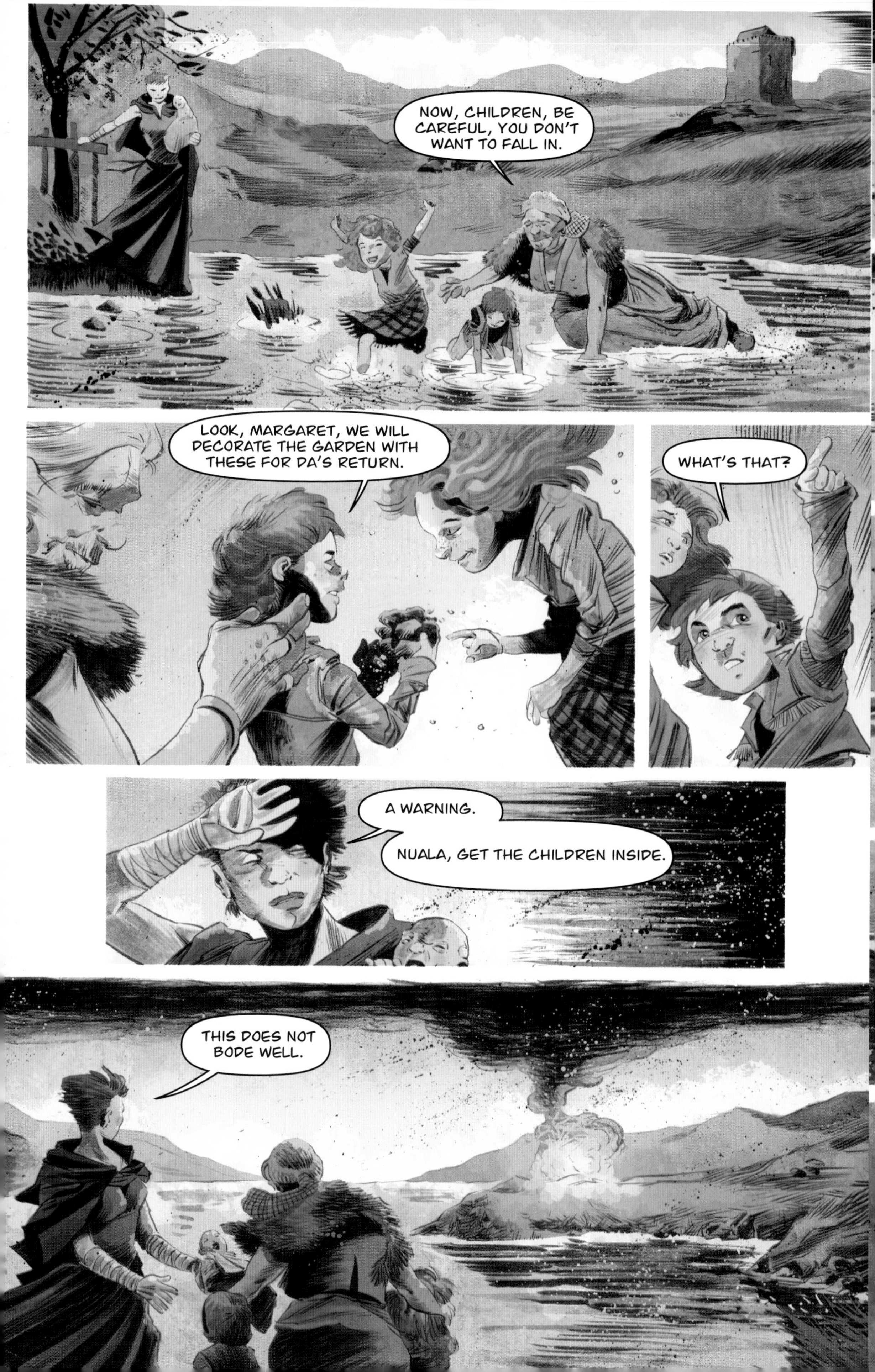
NOW, CHILDREN, BE CAREFUL, YOU DON'T WANT TO FALL IN.
LOOK, MARGARET, WE WILL DECORATE THE GARDEN WITH THESE FOR DA'S RETURN.
WHAT'S THAT?
A WARNING.
NUALA, GET THE CHILDREN INSIDE.
THIS DOES NOT BODE WELL.

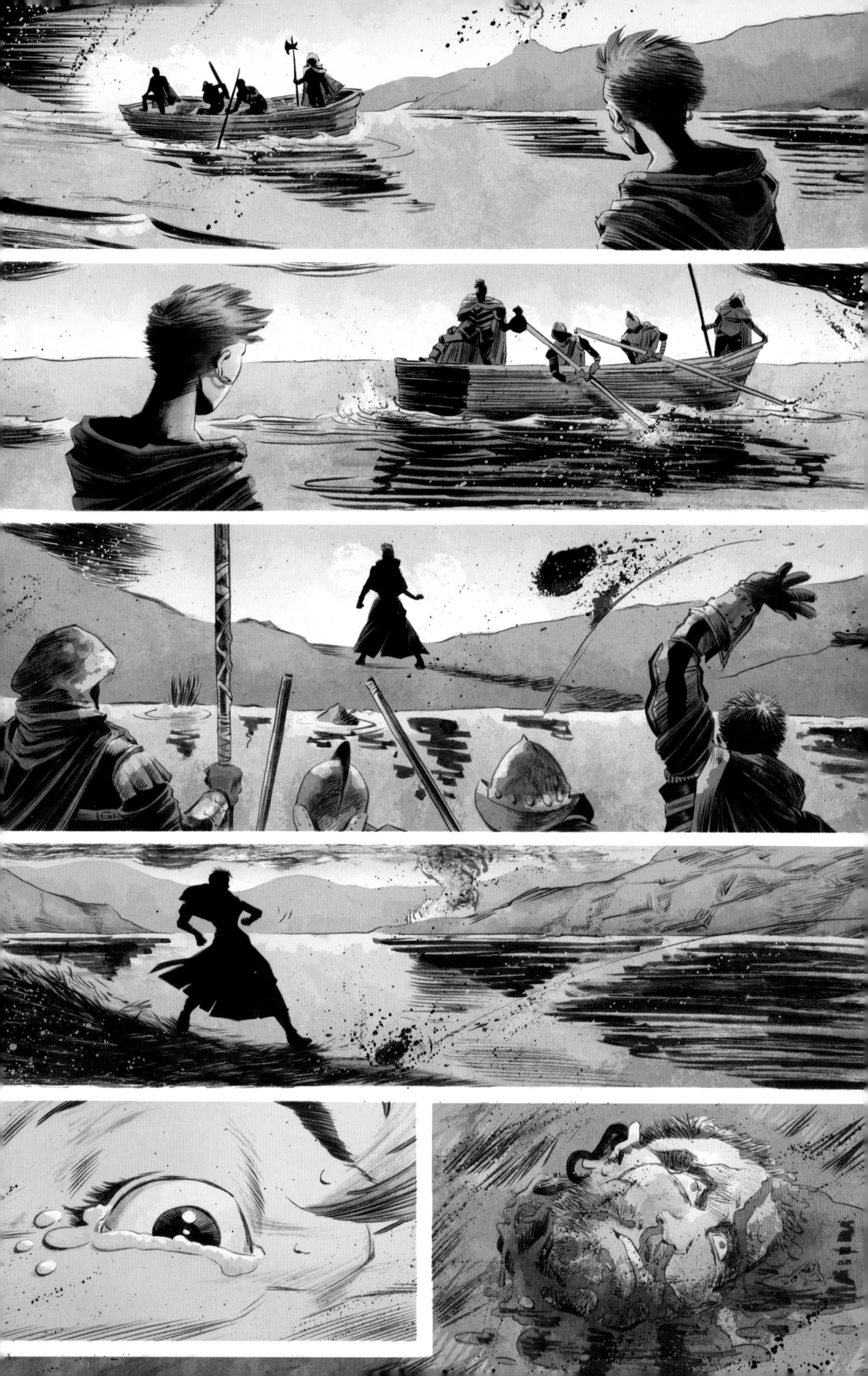

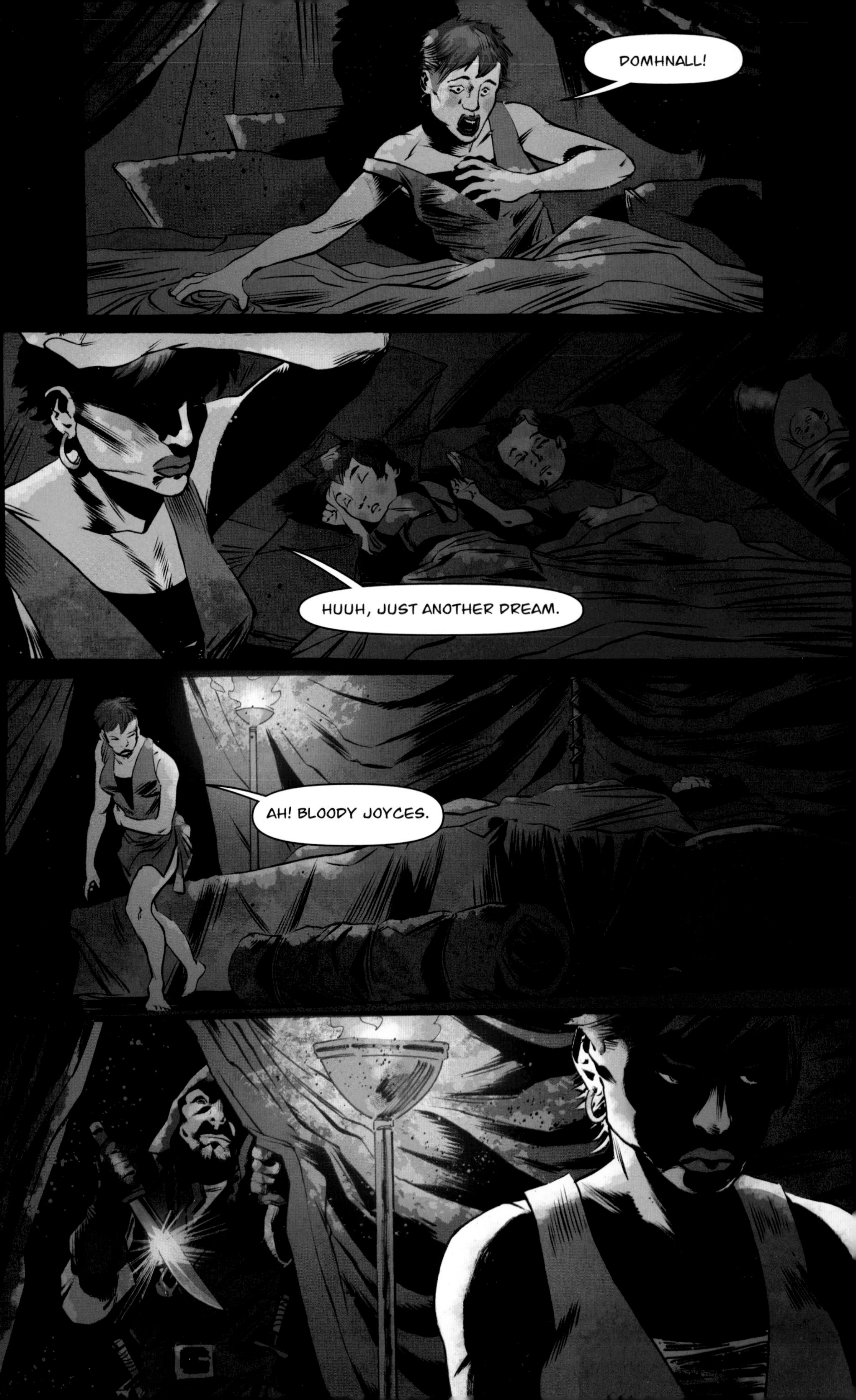
DOMHNALL!
HUUH, JUST ANOTHER DREAM.
AH! BLOODY JOYCES.

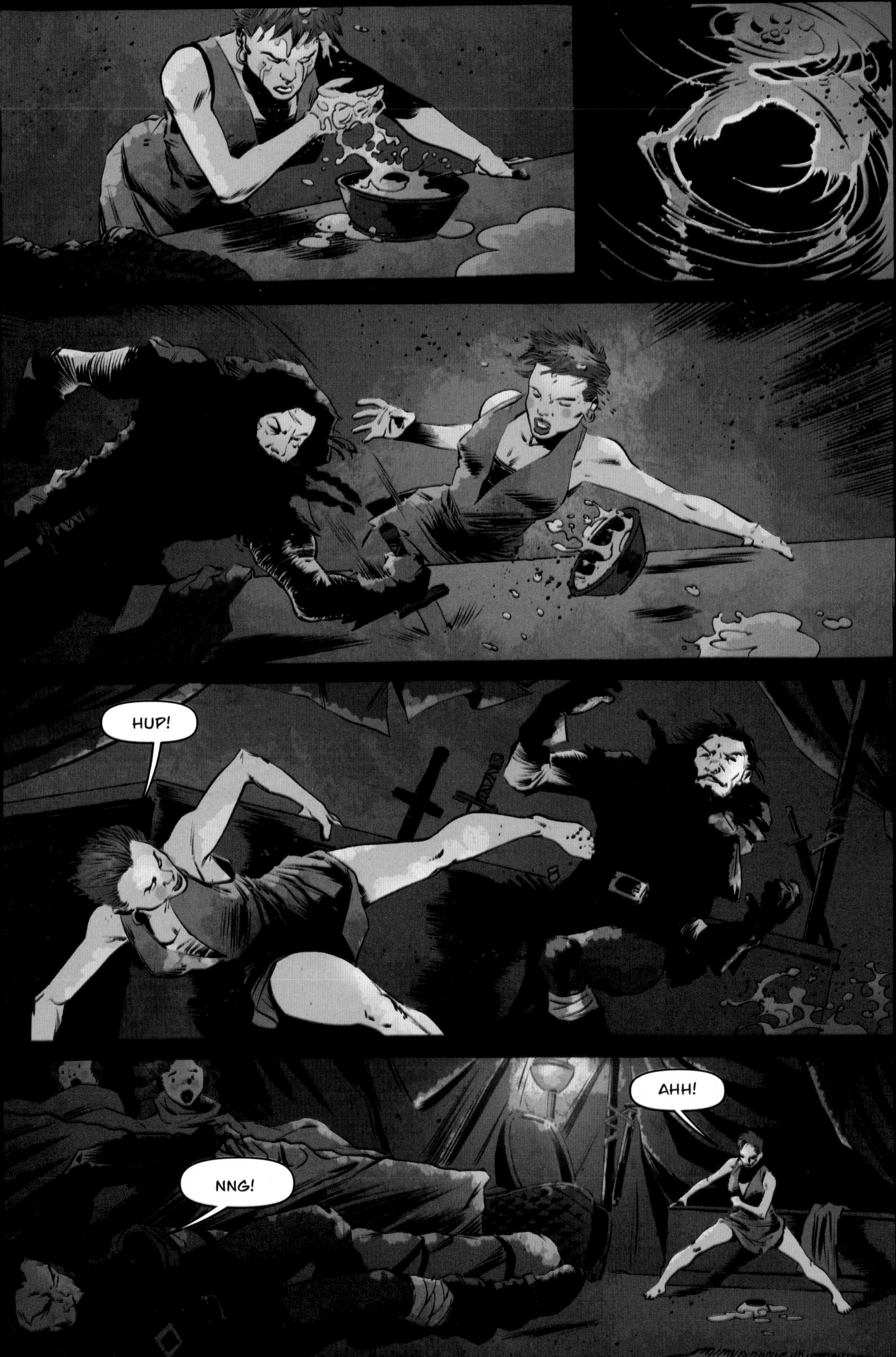
HUP!
AHH!
NNG!

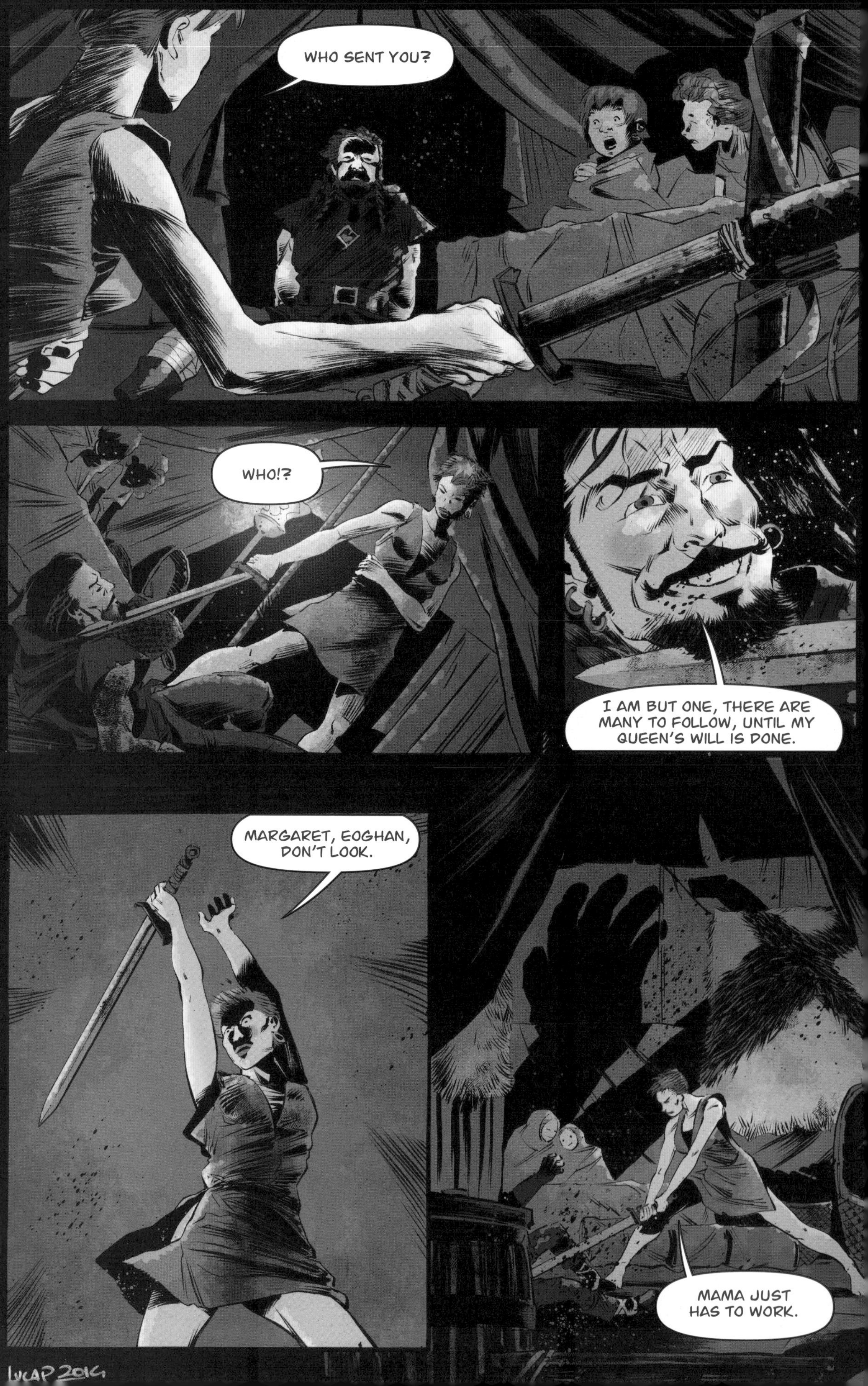
WHO SENT YOU?
WHO!?
I AM BUT ONE, THERE ARE MANY TO FOLLOW, UNTIL MY QUEEN'S WILL IS DONE.
MARGARET, EOGHAN, DON'T LOOK.
MAMA JUST HAS TO WORK.
LUCAP 2016

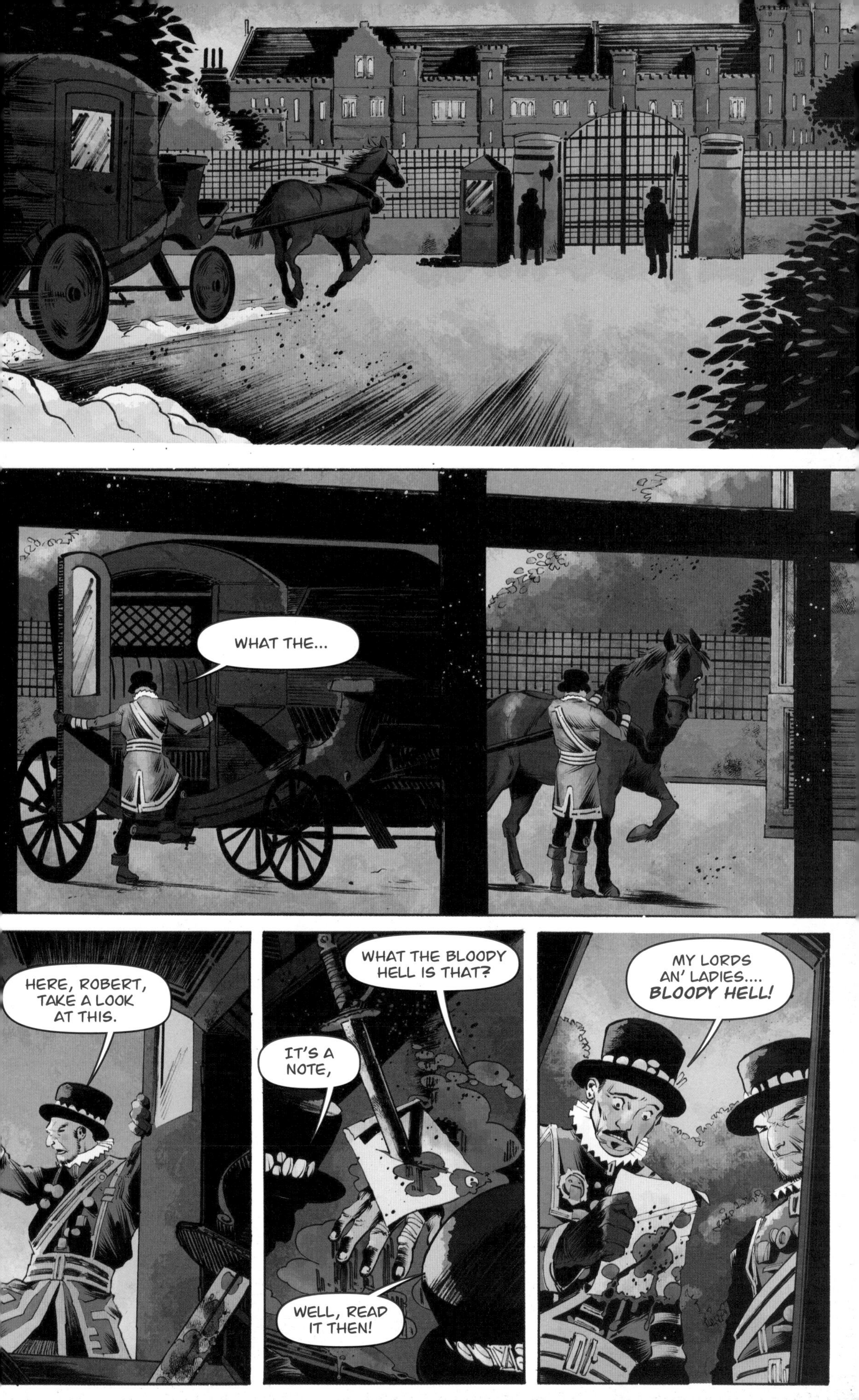

WHAT THE...
HERE, ROBERT, TAKE A LOOK AT THIS.
WHAT THE BLOODY HELL IS THAT?
IT'S A NOTE,
WELL, READ IT THEN!
MY LORDS AN' LADIES.... **BLOODY HELL!**

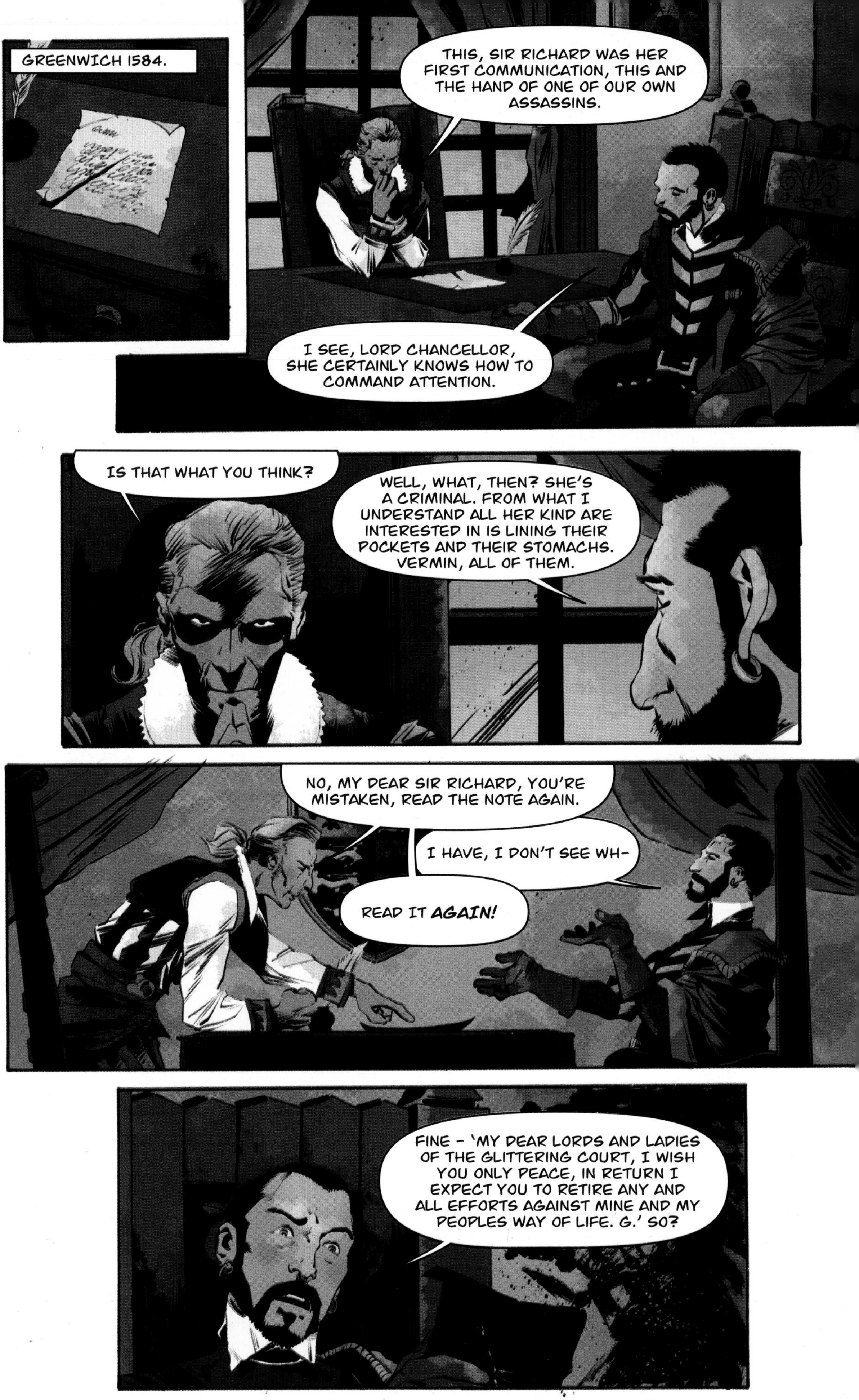
GREENWICH 1584.
THIS, SIR RICHARD WAS HER FIRST COMMUNICATION, THIS AND THE HAND OF ONE OF OUR OWN ASSASSINS.
I SEE, LORD CHANCELLOR, SHE CERTAINLY KNOWS HOW TO COMMAND ATTENTION.
IS THAT WHAT YOU THINK?
WELL, WHAT, THEN? SHE'S A CRIMINAL. FROM WHAT I UNDERSTAND ALL HER KIND ARE INTERESTED IN IS LINING THEIR POCKETS AND THEIR STOMACHS. VERMIN, ALL OF THEM.
NO, MY DEAR SIR RICHARD, YOU'RE MISTAKEN, READ THE NOTE AGAIN.
I HAVE, I DON'T SEE WH-
READ IT **AGAIN!**
FINE – 'MY DEAR LORDS AND LADIES OF THE GLITTERING COURT, I WISH YOU ONLY PEACE, IN RETURN I EXPECT YOU TO RETIRE ANY AND ALL EFFORTS AGAINST MINE AND MY PEOPLES WAY OF LIFE. G.' SO?

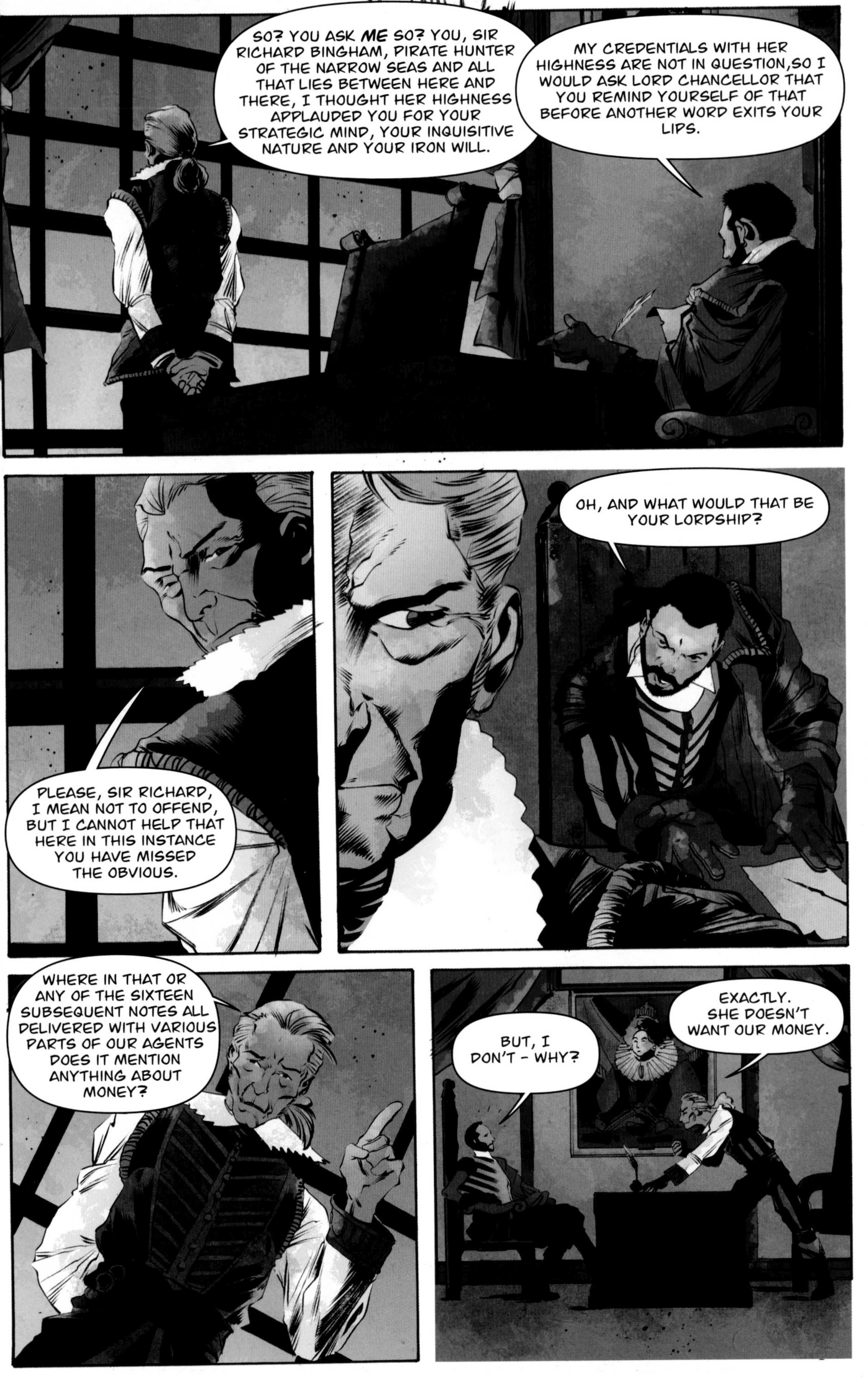
SO? YOU ASK ME SO? YOU, SIR RICHARD BINGHAM, PIRATE HUNTER OF THE NARROW SEAS AND ALL THAT LIES BETWEEN HERE AND THERE, I THOUGHT HER HIGHNESS APPLAUDED YOU FOR YOUR STRATEGIC MIND, YOUR INQUISITIVE NATURE AND YOUR IRON WILL.
MY CREDENTIALS WITH HER HIGHNESS ARE NOT IN QUESTION,SO I WOULD ASK LORD CHANCELLOR THAT YOU REMIND YOURSELF OF THAT BEFORE ANOTHER WORD EXITS YOUR LIPS.
PLEASE, SIR RICHARD, I MEAN NOT TO OFFEND, BUT I CANNOT HELP THAT HERE IN THIS INSTANCE YOU HAVE MISSED THE OBVIOUS.
OH, AND WHAT WOULD THAT BE YOUR LORDSHIP?
WHERE IN THAT OR ANY OF THE SIXTEEN SUBSEQUENT NOTES ALL DELIVERED WITH VARIOUS PARTS OF OUR AGENTS DOES IT MENTION ANYTHING ABOUT MONEY?
BUT, I DON'T - WHY?
EXACTLY. SHE DOESN'T WANT OUR MONEY.

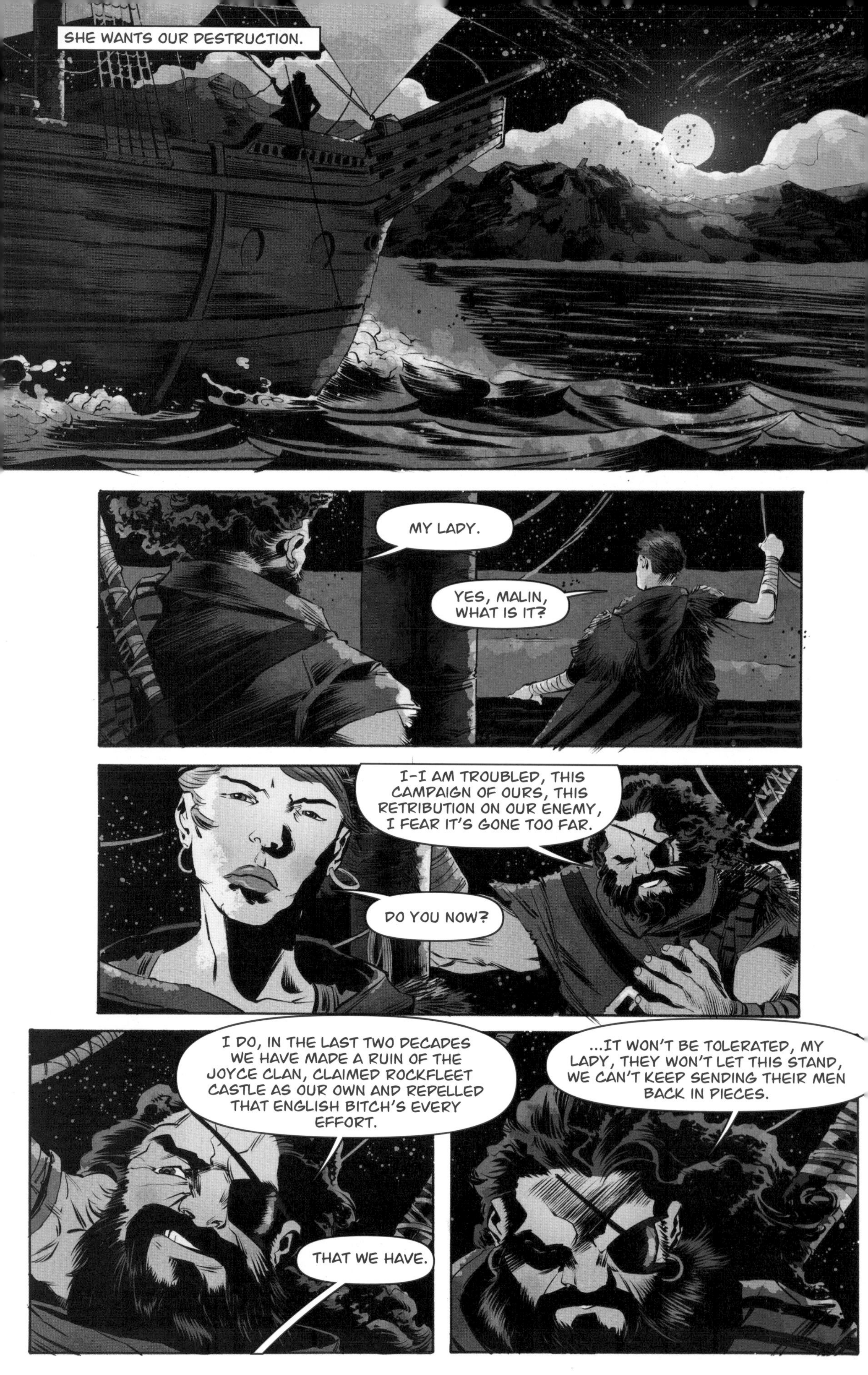
SHE WANTS OUR DESTRUCTION.
MY LADY.
YES, MALIN, WHAT IS IT?
I-I AM TROUBLED, THIS CAMPAIGN OF OURS, THIS RETRIBUTION ON OUR ENEMY, I FEAR IT'S GONE TOO FAR.
DO YOU NOW?
I DO, IN THE LAST TWO DECADES WE HAVE MADE A RUIN OF THE JOYCE CLAN, CLAIMED ROCKFLEET CASTLE AS OUR OWN AND REPELLED THAT ENGLISH BITCH'S EVERY EFFORT.
THAT WE HAVE.
...IT WON'T BE TOLERATED, MY LADY, THEY WON'T LET THIS STAND, WE CAN'T KEEP SENDING THEIR MEN BACK IN PIECES.

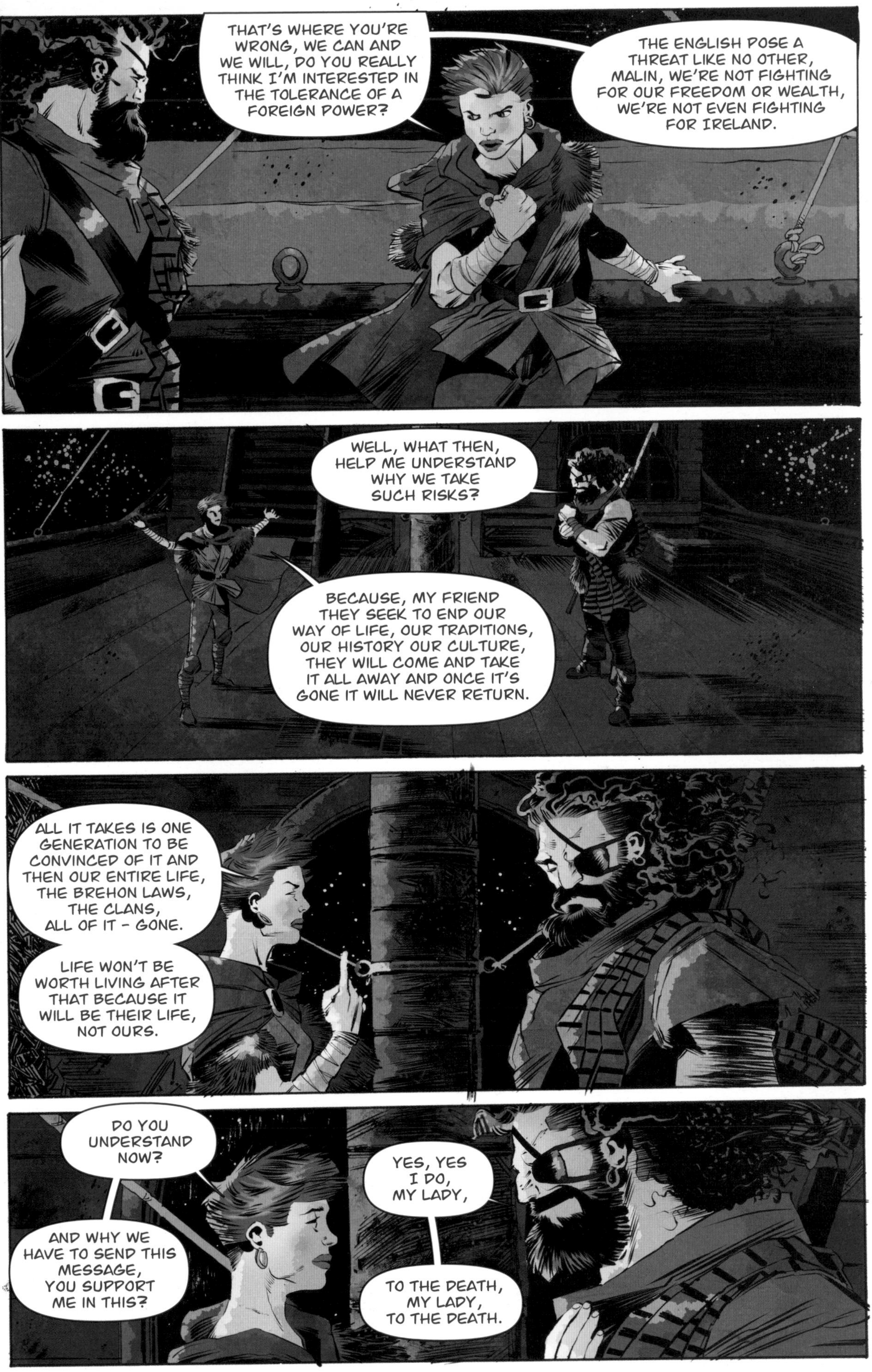
THAT'S WHERE YOU'RE WRONG, WE CAN AND WE WILL, DO YOU REALLY THINK I'M INTERESTED IN THE TOLERANCE OF A FOREIGN POWER?
THE ENGLISH POSE A THREAT LIKE NO OTHER, MALIN, WE'RE NOT FIGHTING FOR OUR FREEDOM OR WEALTH, WE'RE NOT EVEN FIGHTING FOR IRELAND.
WELL, WHAT THEN, HELP ME UNDERSTAND WHY WE TAKE SUCH RISKS?
BECAUSE, MY FRIEND THEY SEEK TO END OUR WAY OF LIFE, OUR TRADITIONS, OUR HISTORY OUR CULTURE, THEY WILL COME AND TAKE IT ALL AWAY AND ONCE IT'S GONE IT WILL NEVER RETURN.
ALL IT TAKES IS ONE GENERATION TO BE CONVINCED OF IT AND THEN OUR ENTIRE LIFE, THE BREHON LAWS, THE CLANS, ALL OF IT - GONE.
LIFE WON'T BE WORTH LIVING AFTER THAT BECAUSE IT WILL BE THEIR LIFE, NOT OURS.
DO YOU UNDERSTAND NOW?
AND WHY WE HAVE TO SEND THIS MESSAGE, YOU SUPPORT ME IN THIS?
YES, YES I DO, MY LADY,
TO THE DEATH, MY LADY, TO THE DEATH.

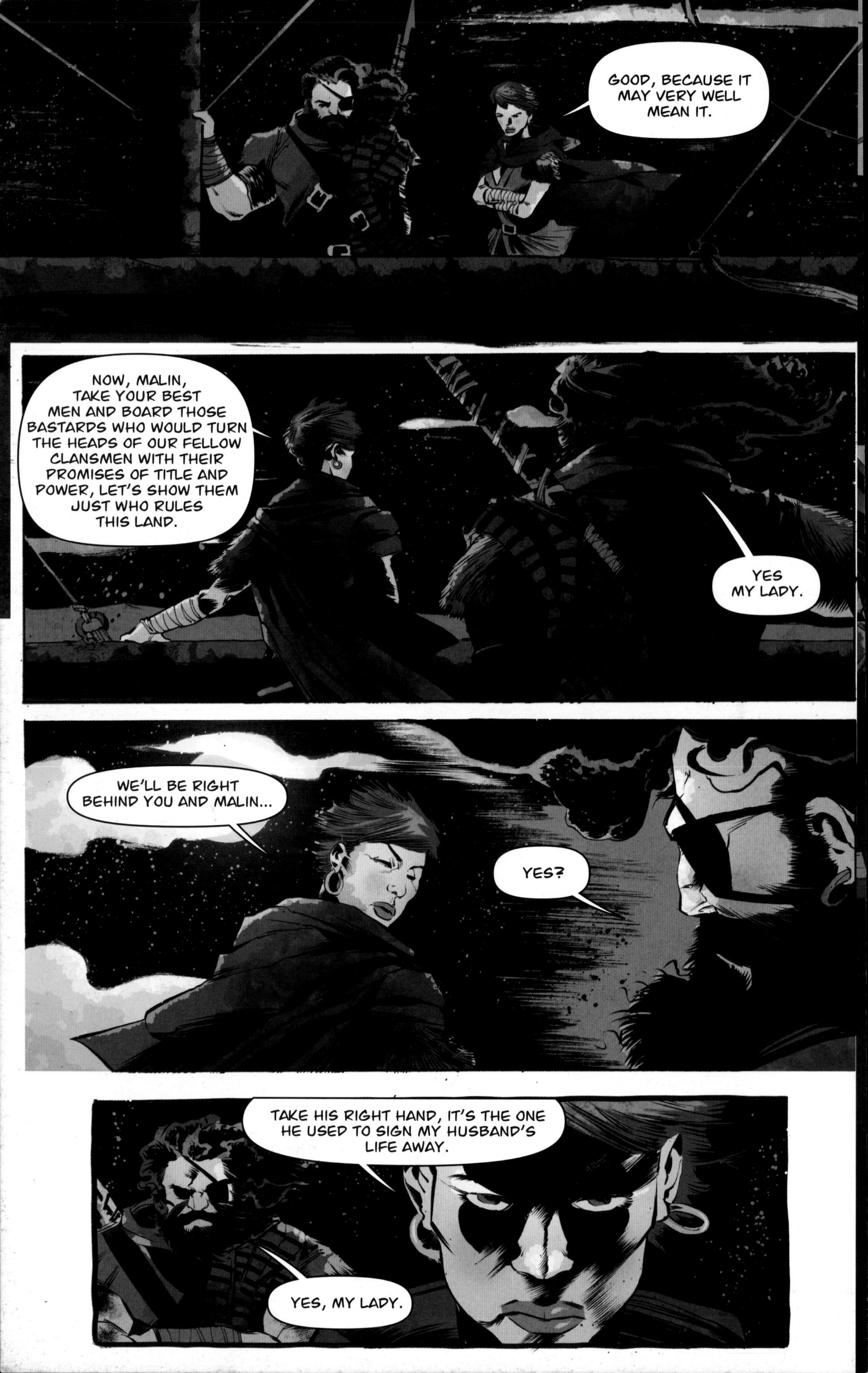
GOOD, BECAUSE IT MAY VERY WELL MEAN IT.
NOW, MALIN, TAKE YOUR BEST MEN AND BOARD THOSE BASTARDS WHO WOULD TURN THE HEADS OF OUR FELLOW CLANSMEN WITH THEIR PROMISES OF TITLE AND POWER, LET'S SHOW THEM JUST WHO RULES THIS LAND.
YES MY LADY.
WE'LL BE RIGHT BEHIND YOU AND MALIN...
YES?
TAKE HIS RIGHT HAND, IT'S THE ONE HE USED TO SIGN MY HUSBAND'S LIFE AWAY.
YES, MY LADY.

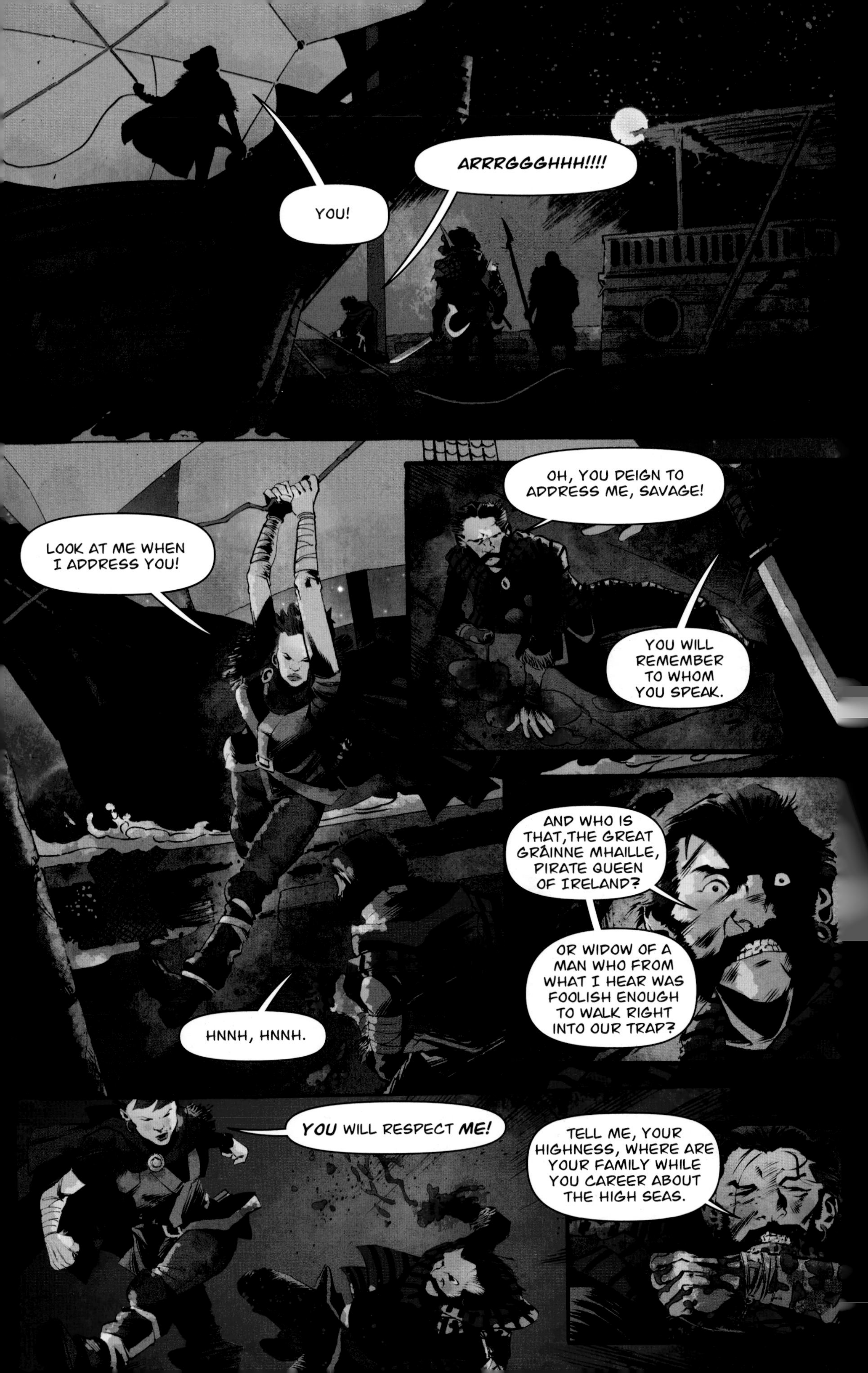
YOU!
ARRRGGGHHH!!!!
LOOK AT ME WHEN I ADDRESS YOU!
OH, YOU DEIGN TO ADDRESS ME, SAVAGE!
YOU WILL REMEMBER TO WHOM YOU SPEAK.
AND WHO IS THAT, THE GREAT GRÂINNE MHAILLE, PIRATE QUEEN OF IRELAND?
OR WIDOW OF A MAN WHO FROM WHAT I HEAR WAS FOOLISH ENOUGH TO WALK RIGHT INTO OUR TRAP?
HNNH, HNNH.
YOU WILL RESPECT ME!
TELL ME, YOUR HIGHNESS, WHERE ARE YOUR FAMILY WHILE YOU CAREER ABOUT THE HIGH SEAS.

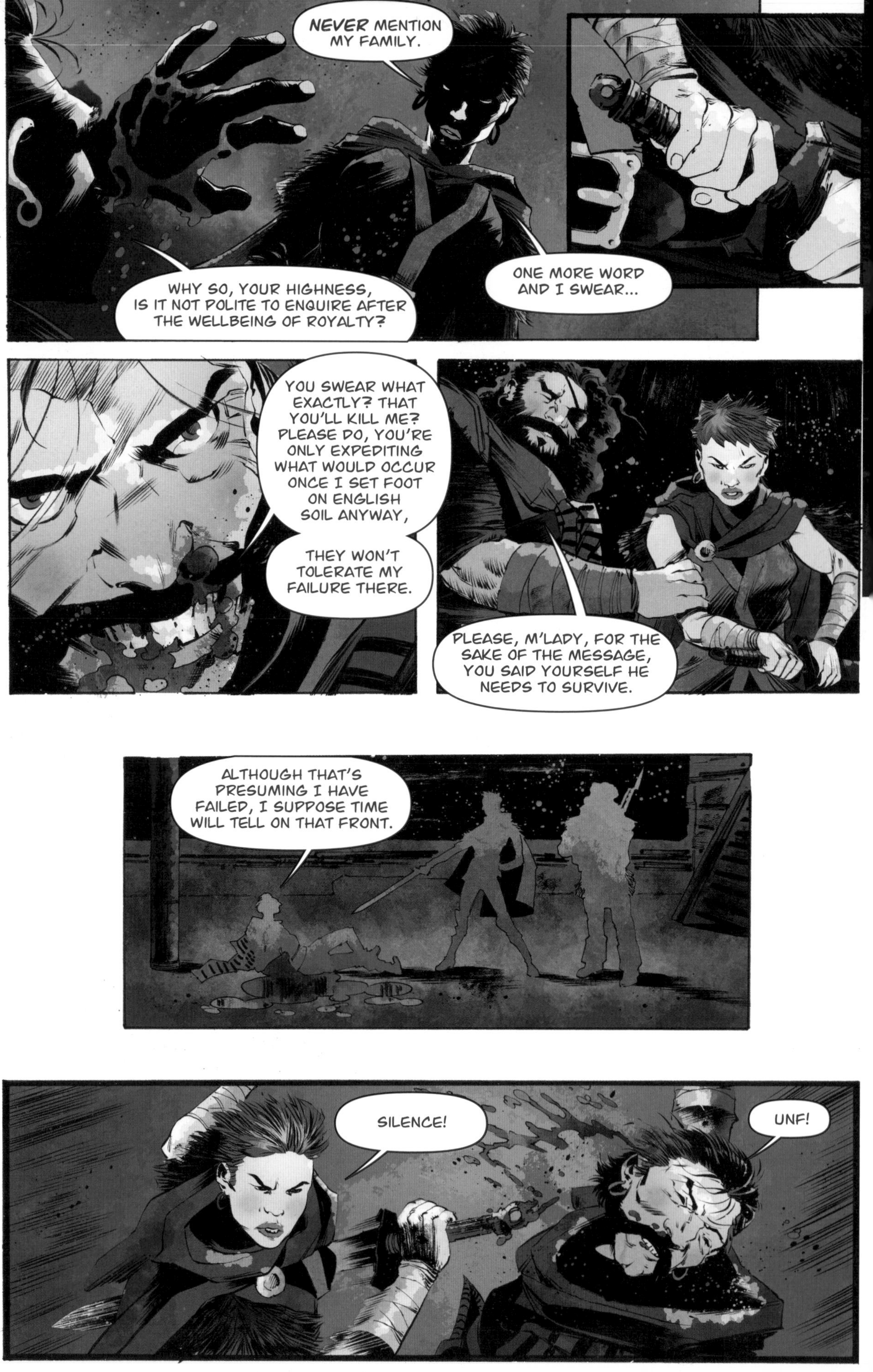
NEVER MENTION MY FAMILY.
WHY SO, YOUR HIGHNESS, IS IT NOT POLITE TO ENQUIRE AFTER THE WELLBEING OF ROYALTY?
ONE MORE WORD AND I SWEAR...
YOU SWEAR WHAT EXACTLY? THAT YOU'LL KILL ME? PLEASE DO, YOU'RE ONLY EXPEDITING WHAT WOULD OCCUR ONCE I SET FOOT ON ENGLISH SOIL ANYWAY,
THEY WON'T TOLERATE MY FAILURE THERE.
PLEASE, M'LADY, FOR THE SAKE OF THE MESSAGE, YOU SAID YOURSELF HE NEEDS TO SURVIVE.
ALTHOUGH THAT'S PRESUMING I HAVE FAILED, I SUPPOSE TIME WILL TELL ON THAT FRONT.
SILENCE!
UNF!

GREENWICH PORT.

THAT WAS THE START OF IT THOUGH,

AYE, I SUPPOSE IT WAS, YOU DON'T MUTILATE A KNIGHT OF THE REALM AND JUST EXPECT TO GET AWAY WITH IT.

AH, BUT ALL THOSE ASSASSINS, AND IT WAS HE THAT CAUGHT HER ATTENTION?

KILL ALL THE LOWBORN YOU LIKE, BUT NOBLEMEN LIKE YER MAN AND YER WELL AND TRULY NOTICED. WHAT WAS HIS NAME?

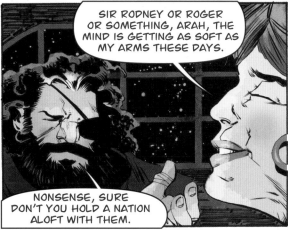

SIR RODNEY OR ROGER OR SOMETHING, ARAH, THE MIND IS GETTING AS SOFT AS MY ARMS THESE DAYS.

NONSENSE, SURE DON'T YOU HOLD A NATION ALOFT WITH THEM.

AH, GO AWAY FROM ME, MALIN! BESIDES THERE ARE PLENTY WHO THINK OTHERWISE ...

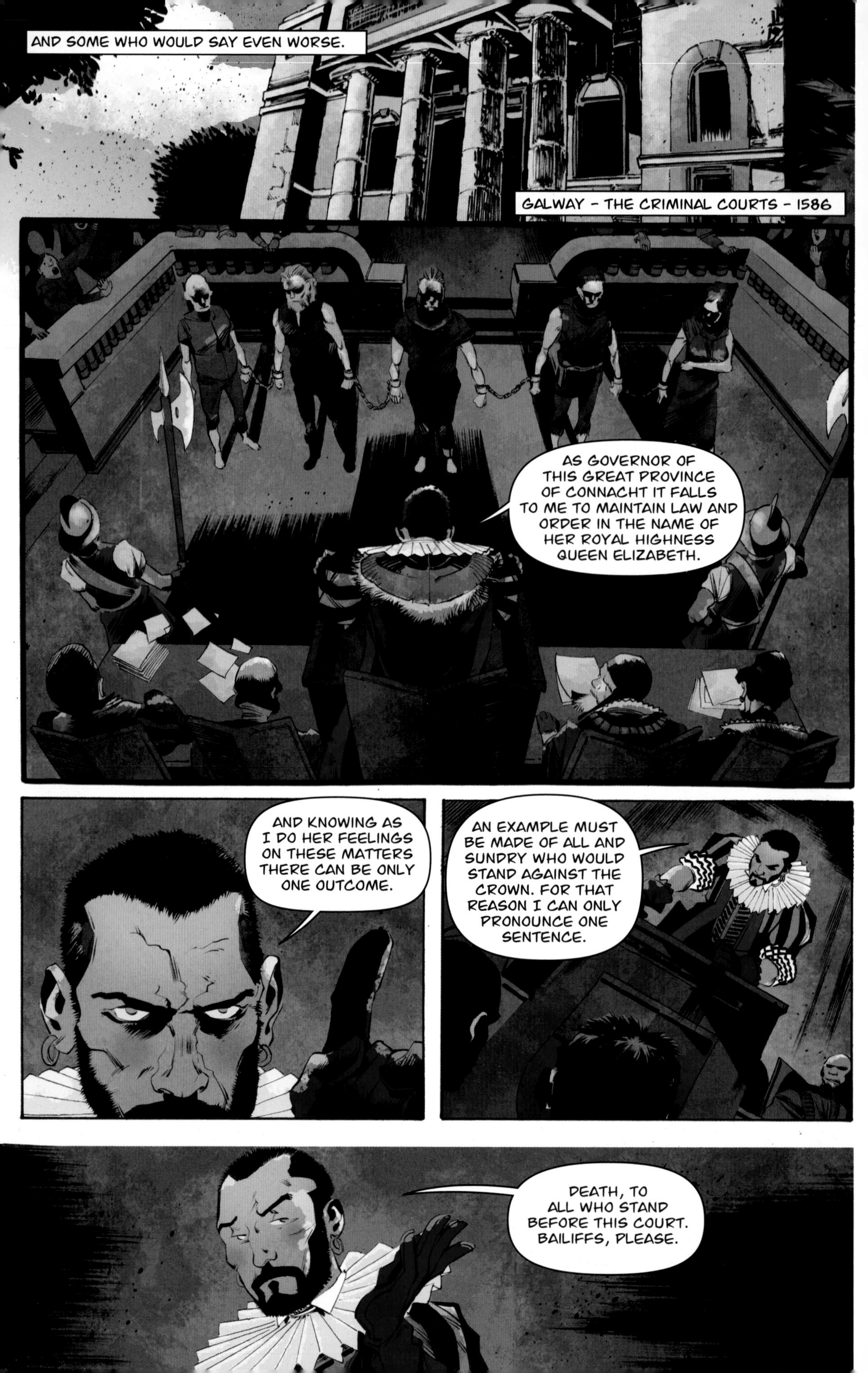
AND SOME WHO WOULD SAY EVEN WORSE.
GALWAY – THE CRIMINAL COURTS – 1586
AS GOVERNOR OF THIS GREAT PROVINCE OF CONNACHT IT FALLS TO ME TO MAINTAIN LAW AND ORDER IN THE NAME OF HER ROYAL HIGHNESS QUEEN ELIZABETH.
AND KNOWING AS I DO HER FEELINGS ON THESE MATTERS THERE CAN BE ONLY ONE OUTCOME.
AN EXAMPLE MUST BE MADE OF ALL AND SUNDRY WHO WOULD STAND AGAINST THE CROWN. FOR THAT REASON I CAN ONLY PRONOUNCE ONE SENTENCE.
DEATH, TO ALL WHO STAND BEFORE THIS COURT. BAILIFFS, PLEASE.

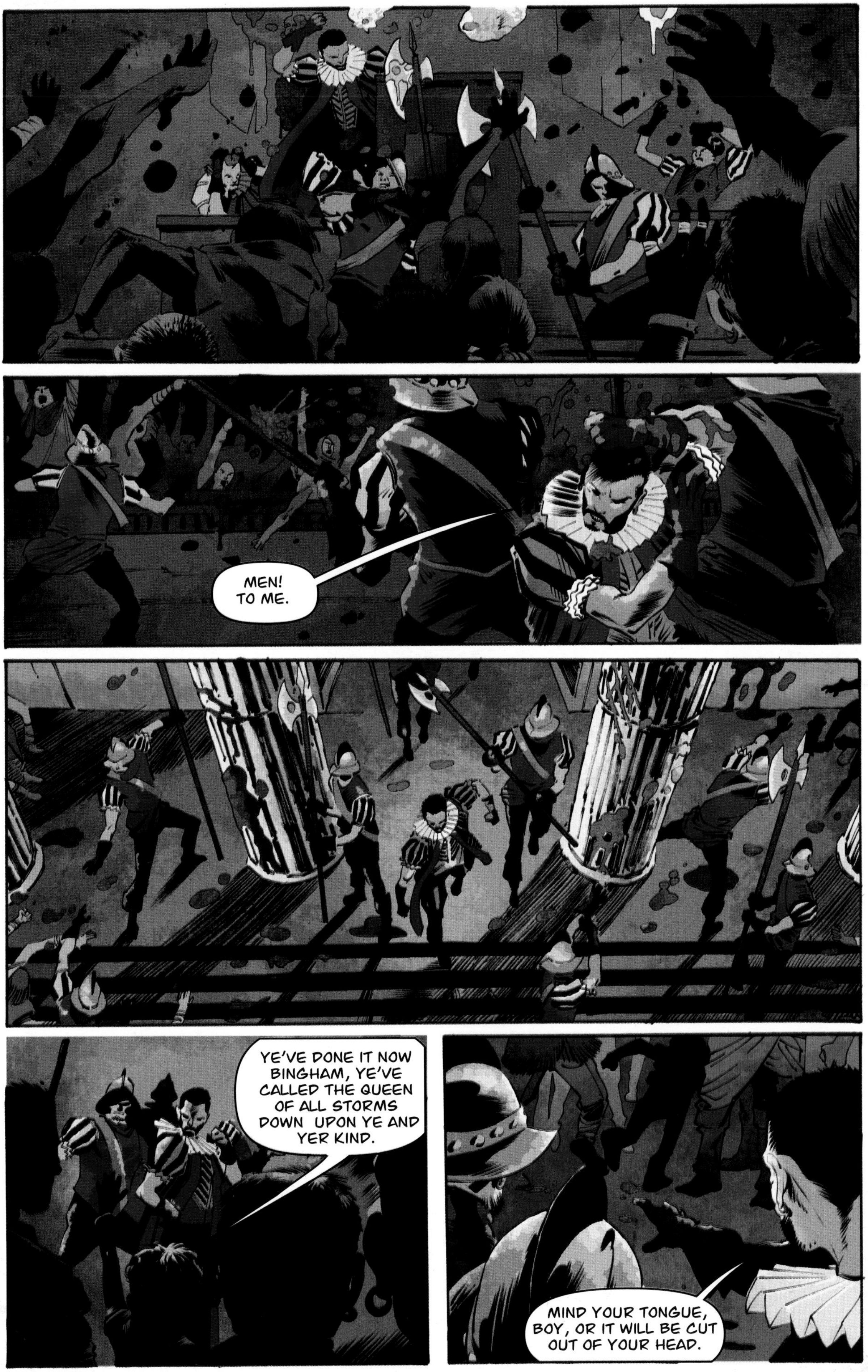
MEN! TO ME.
YE'VE DONE IT NOW BINGHAM, YE'VE CALLED THE QUEEN OF ALL STORMS DOWN UPON YE AND YER KIND.
MIND YOUR TONGUE, BOY, OR IT WILL BE CUT OUT OF YOUR HEAD.

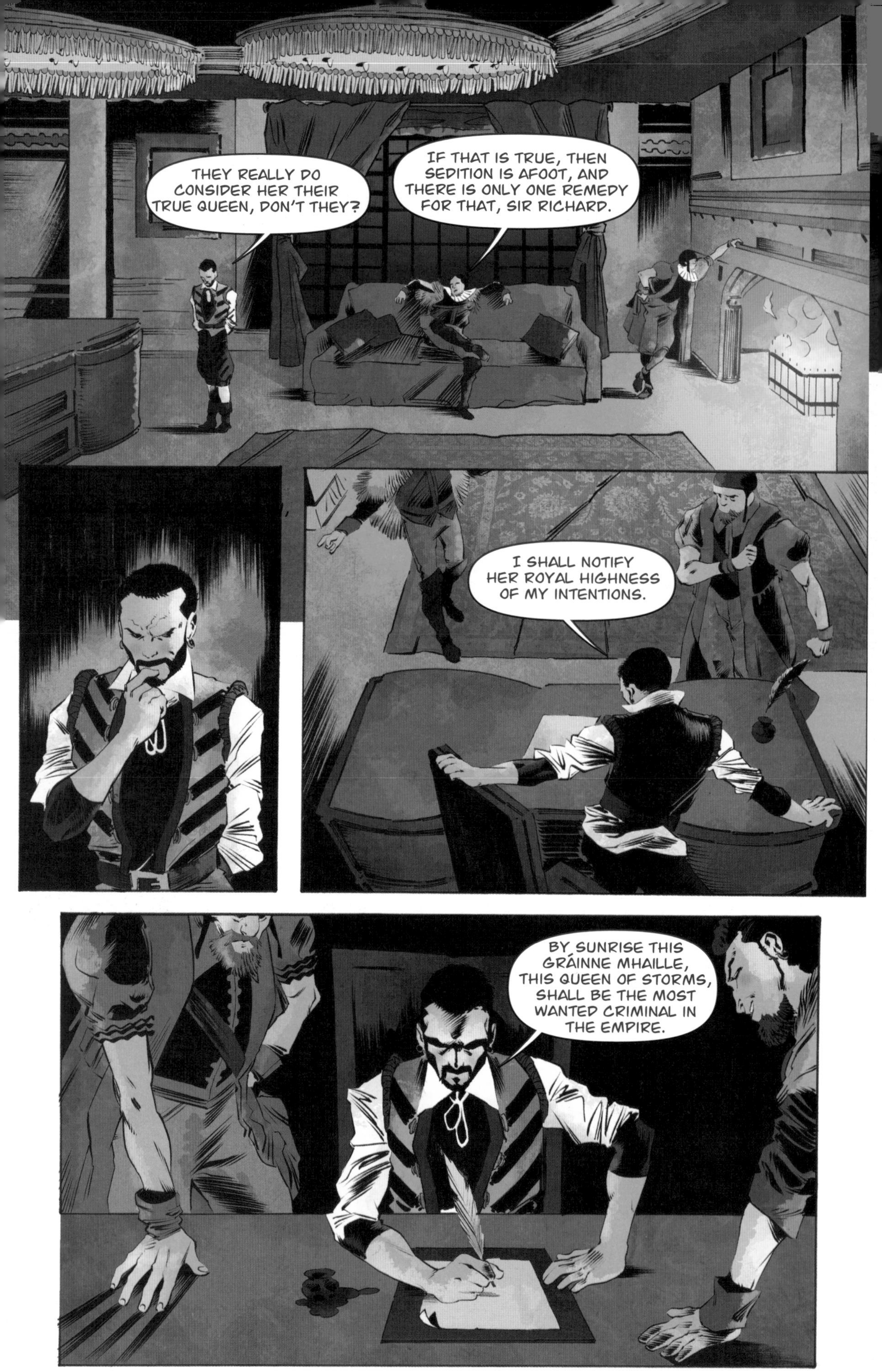
THEY REALLY DO CONSIDER HER THEIR TRUE QUEEN, DON'T THEY?
IF THAT IS TRUE, THEN SEDITION IS AFOOT, AND THERE IS ONLY ONE REMEDY FOR THAT, SIR RICHARD.
I SHALL NOTIFY HER ROYAL HIGHNESS OF MY INTENTIONS.
BY SUNRISE THIS GRÁINNE MHAILLE, THIS QUEEN OF STORMS, SHALL BE THE MOST WANTED CRIMINAL IN THE EMPIRE.

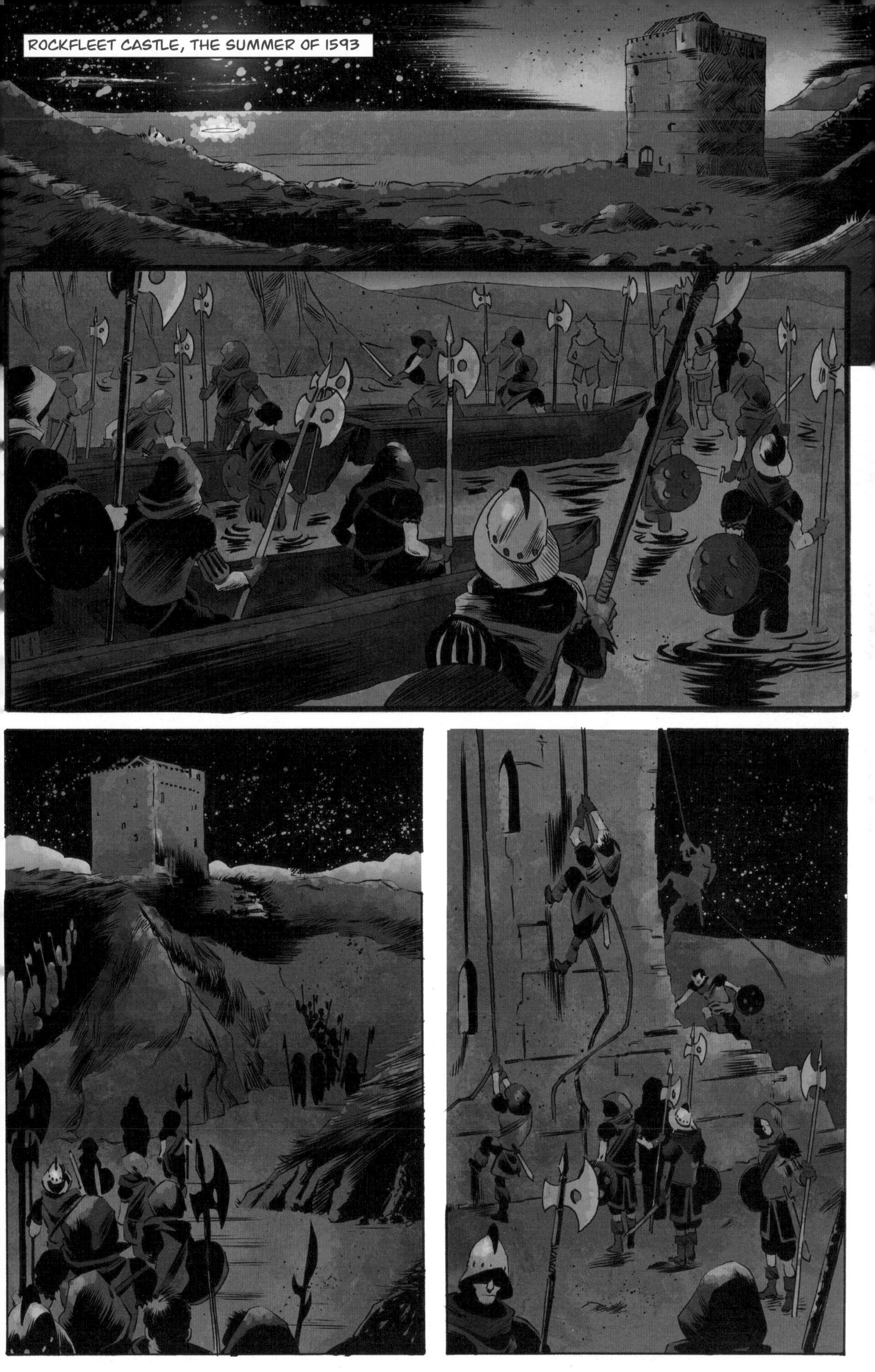
ROCKFLEET CASTLE, THE SUMMER OF 1593

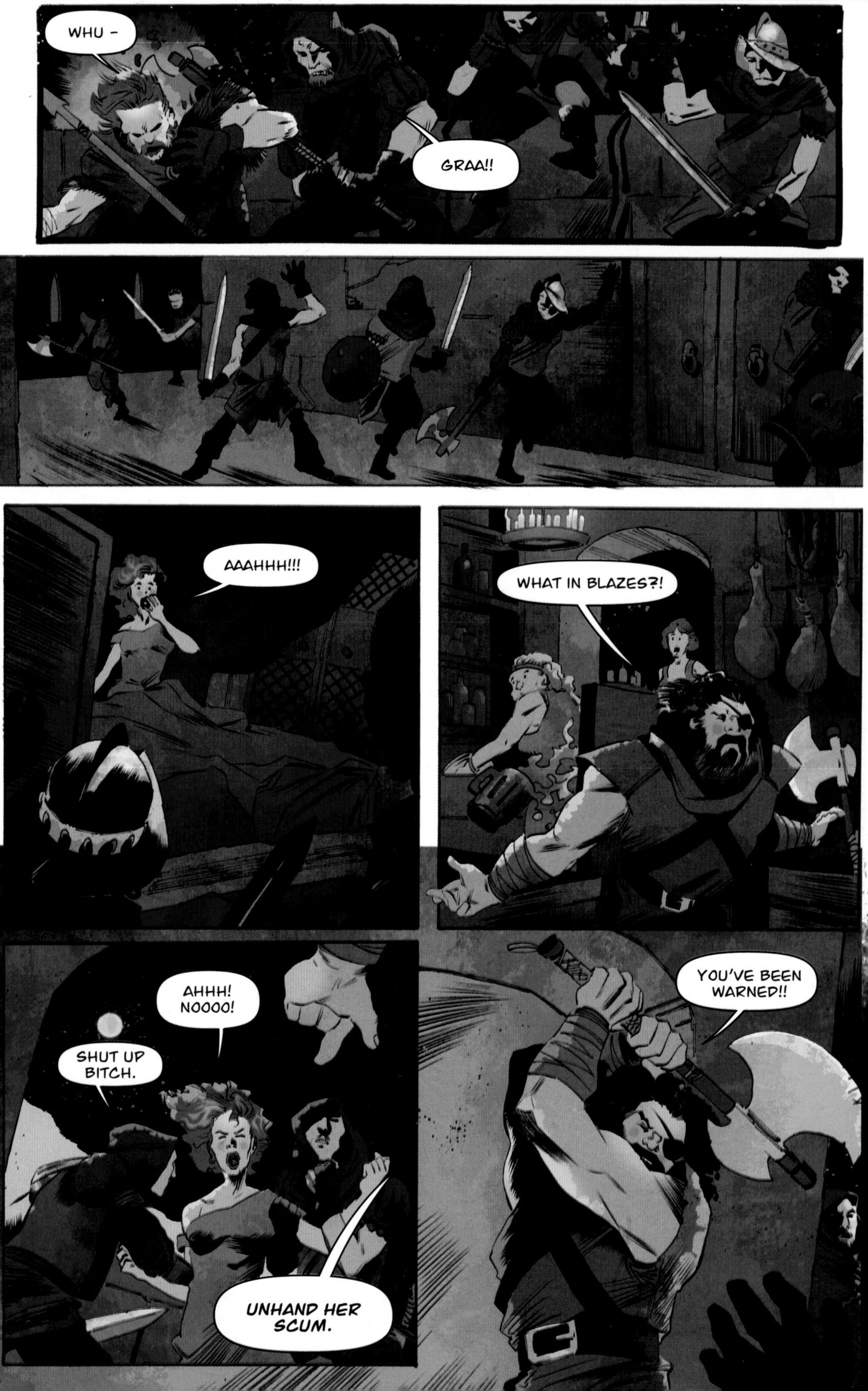
WHU -
GRAA!!
AAAHHH!!!
WHAT IN BLAZES?!
AHHH! NOOOO!
SHUT UP BITCH.
UNHAND HER SCUM.
YOU'VE BEEN WARNED!!

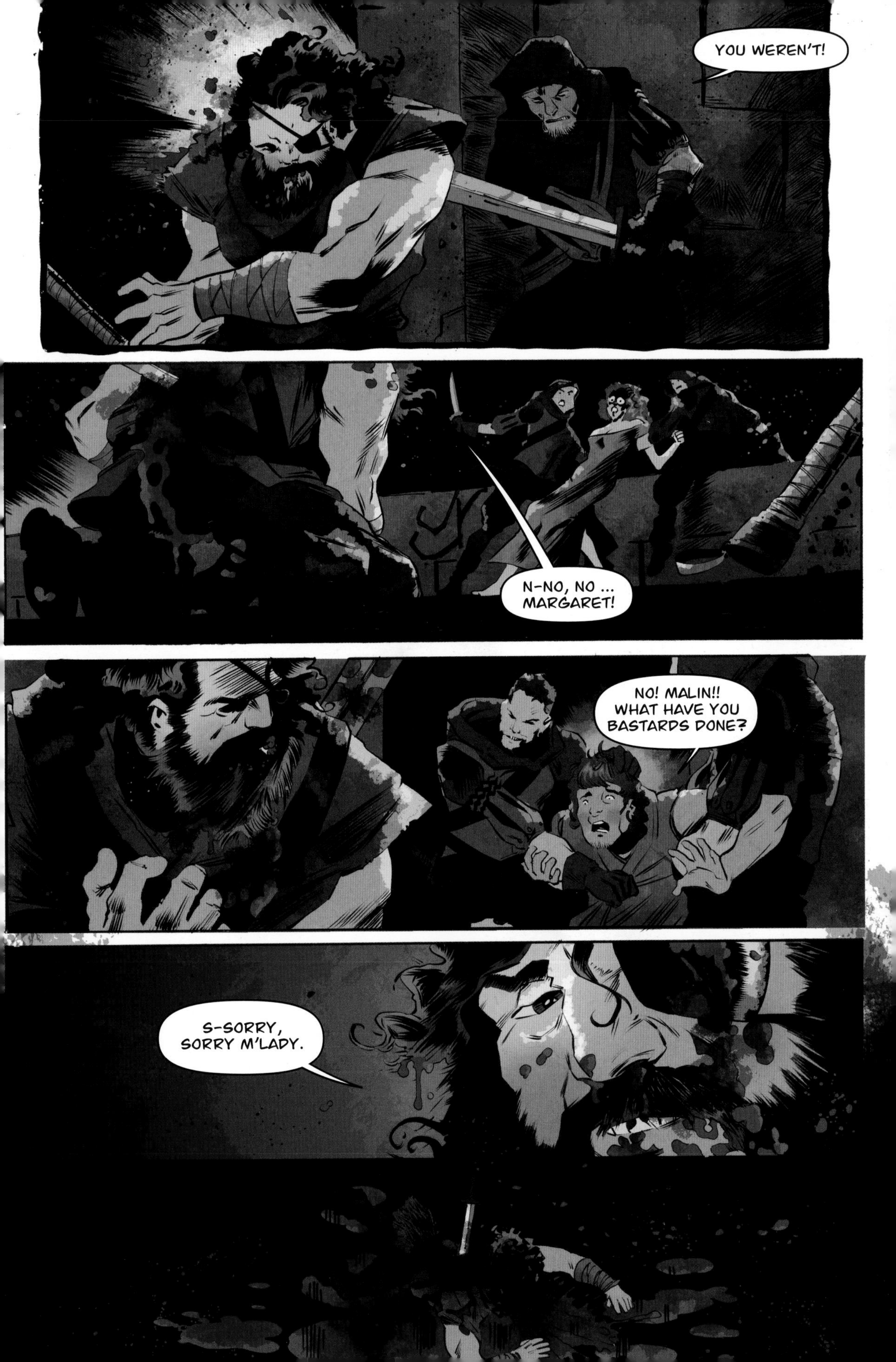
YOU WEREN'T!
N-NO, NO ...
MARGARET!
NO! MALIN!!
WHAT HAVE YOU
BASTARDS DONE?
S-SORRY,
SORRY M'LADY.

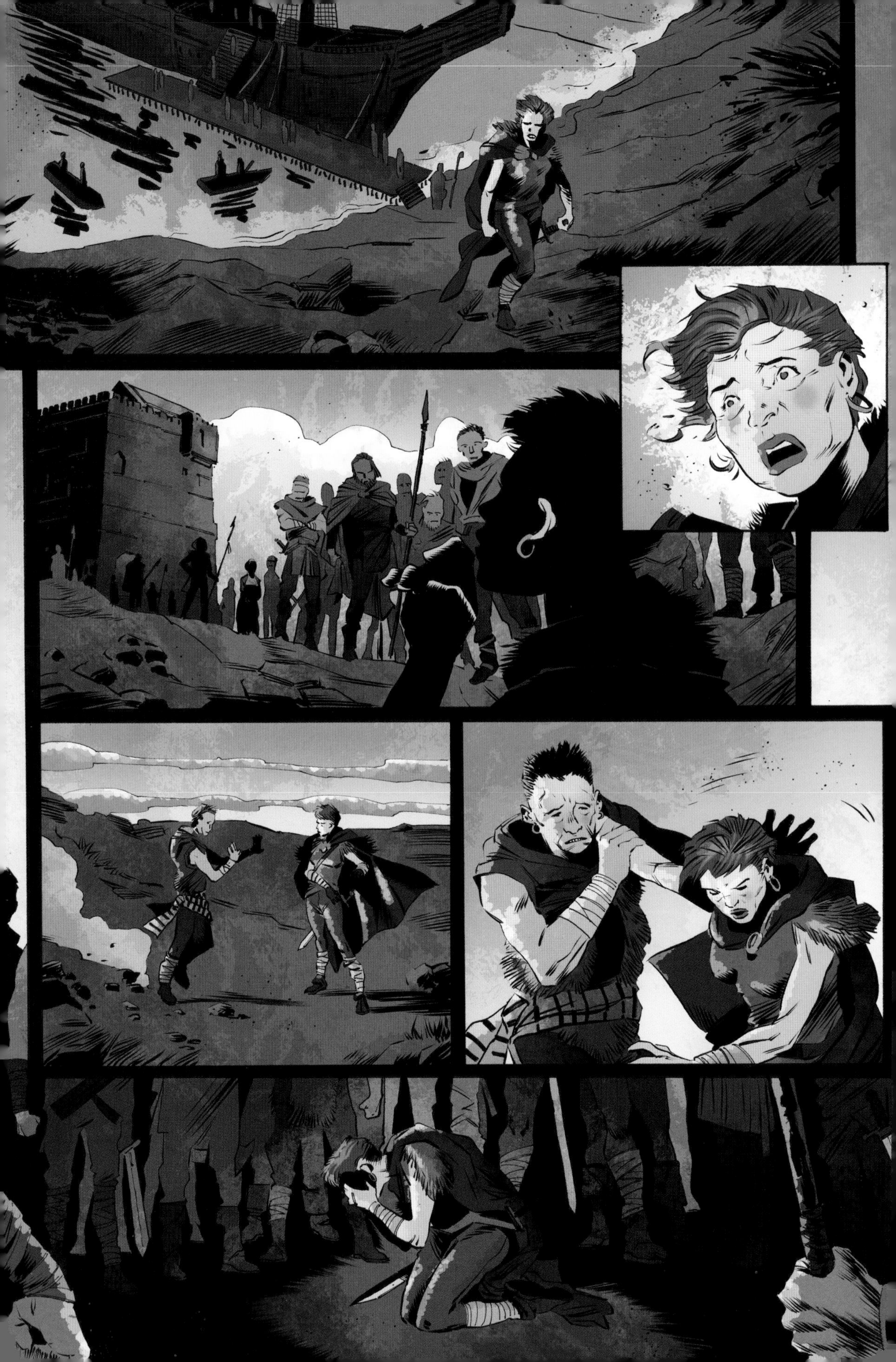

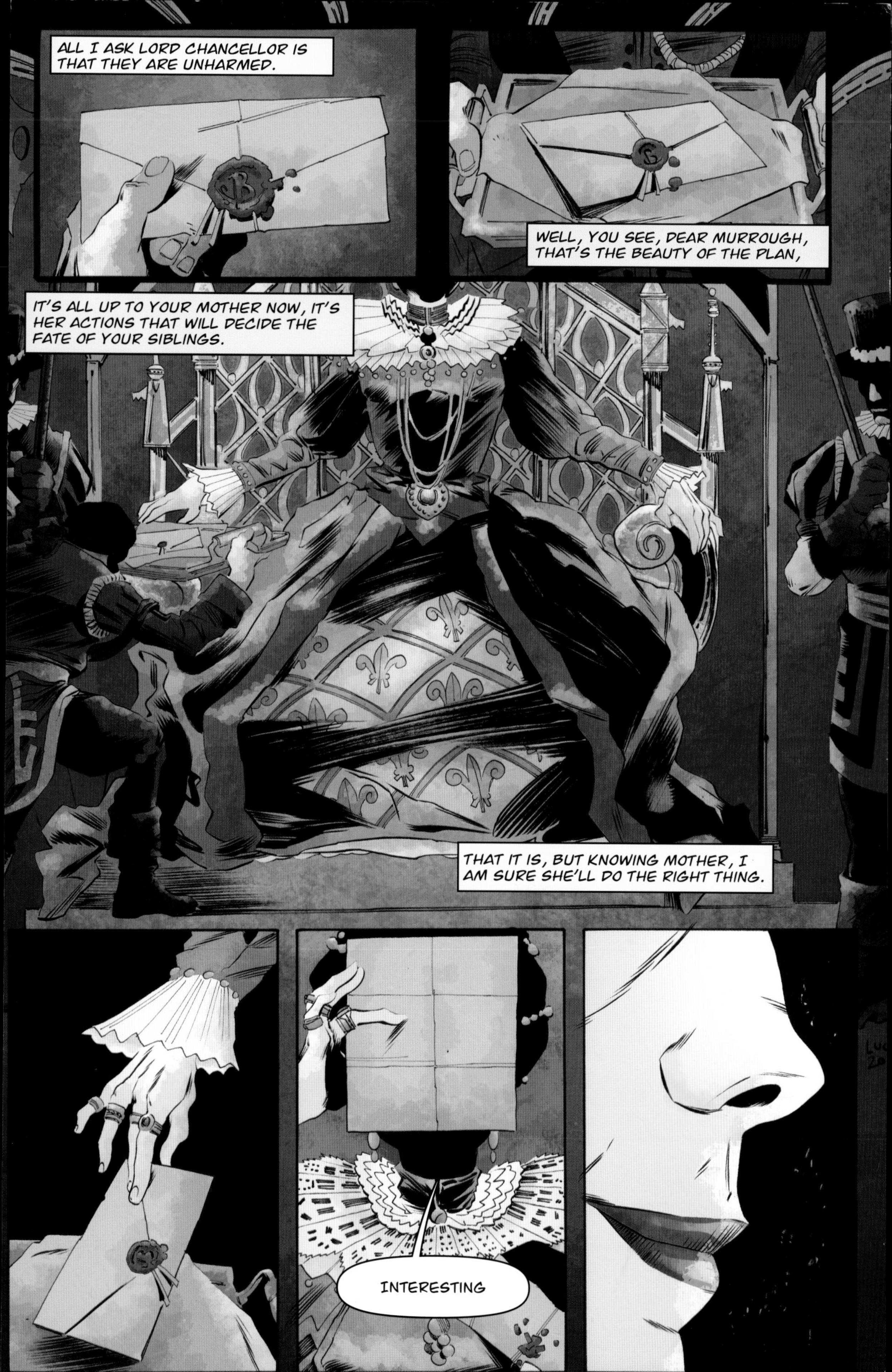
ALL I ASK LORD CHANCELLOR IS THAT THEY ARE UNHARMED.
WELL, YOU SEE, DEAR MURROUGH, THAT'S THE BEAUTY OF THE PLAN,
IT'S ALL UP TO YOUR MOTHER NOW, IT'S HER ACTIONS THAT WILL DECIDE THE FATE OF YOUR SIBLINGS.
THAT IT IS, BUT KNOWING MOTHER, I AM SURE SHE'LL DO THE RIGHT THING.
INTERESTING

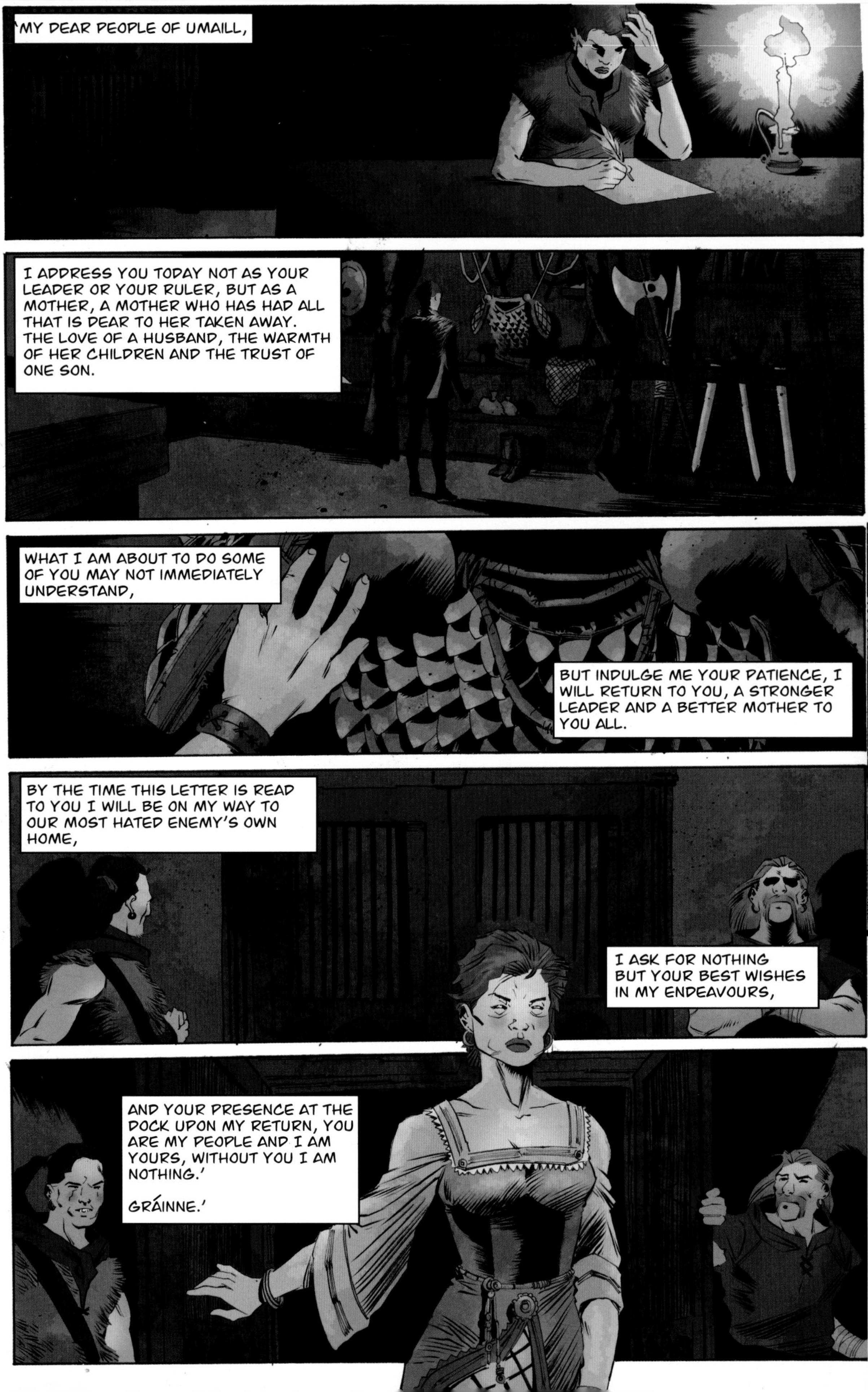
'MY DEAR PEOPLE OF UMAILL,
I ADDRESS YOU TODAY NOT AS YOUR LEADER OR YOUR RULER, BUT AS A MOTHER, A MOTHER WHO HAS HAD ALL THAT IS DEAR TO HER TAKEN AWAY. THE LOVE OF A HUSBAND, THE WARMTH OF HER CHILDREN AND THE TRUST OF ONE SON.
WHAT I AM ABOUT TO DO SOME OF YOU MAY NOT IMMEDIATELY UNDERSTAND,
BUT INDULGE ME YOUR PATIENCE, I WILL RETURN TO YOU, A STRONGER LEADER AND A BETTER MOTHER TO YOU ALL.
BY THE TIME THIS LETTER IS READ TO YOU I WILL BE ON MY WAY TO OUR MOST HATED ENEMY'S OWN HOME,
I ASK FOR NOTHING BUT YOUR BEST WISHES IN MY ENDEAVOURS,
AND YOUR PRESENCE AT THE DOCK UPON MY RETURN, YOU ARE MY PEOPLE AND I AM YOURS, WITHOUT YOU I AM NOTHING.'
GRÁINNE.'

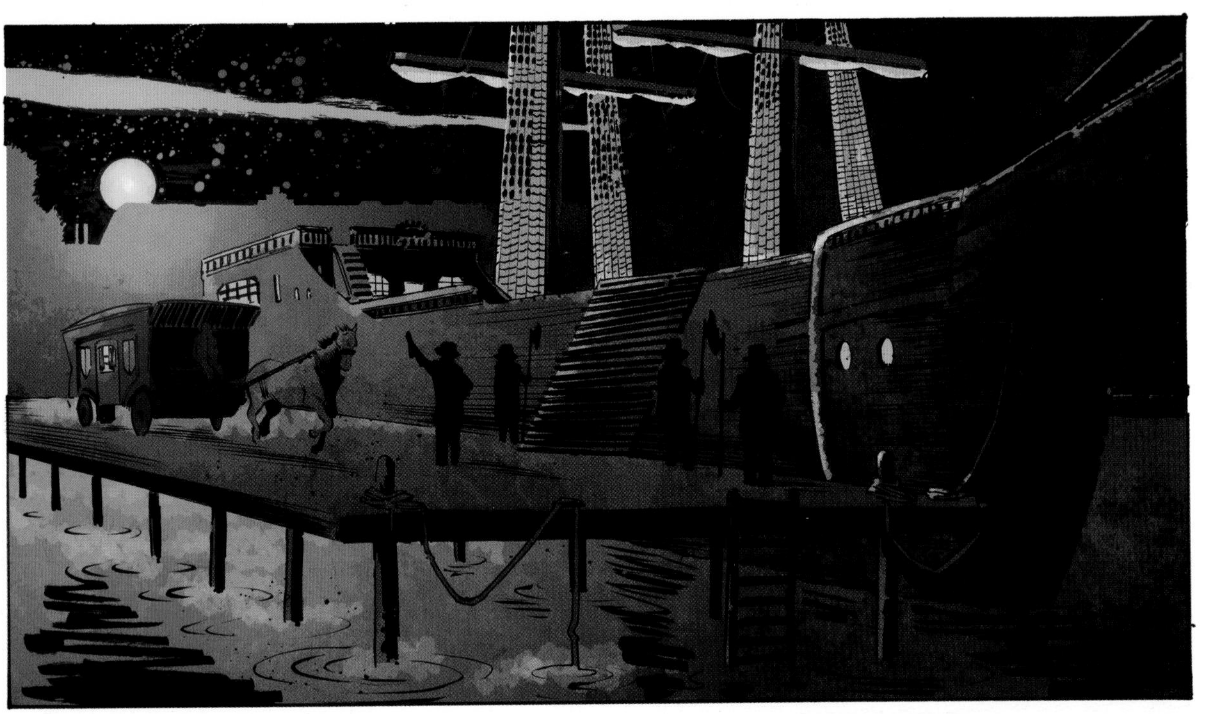

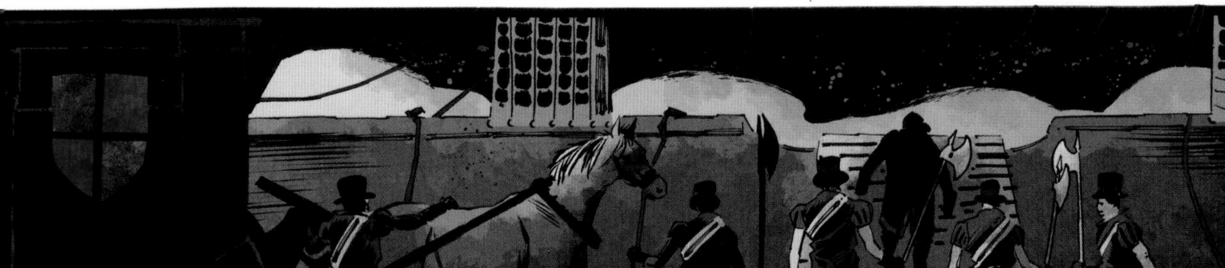

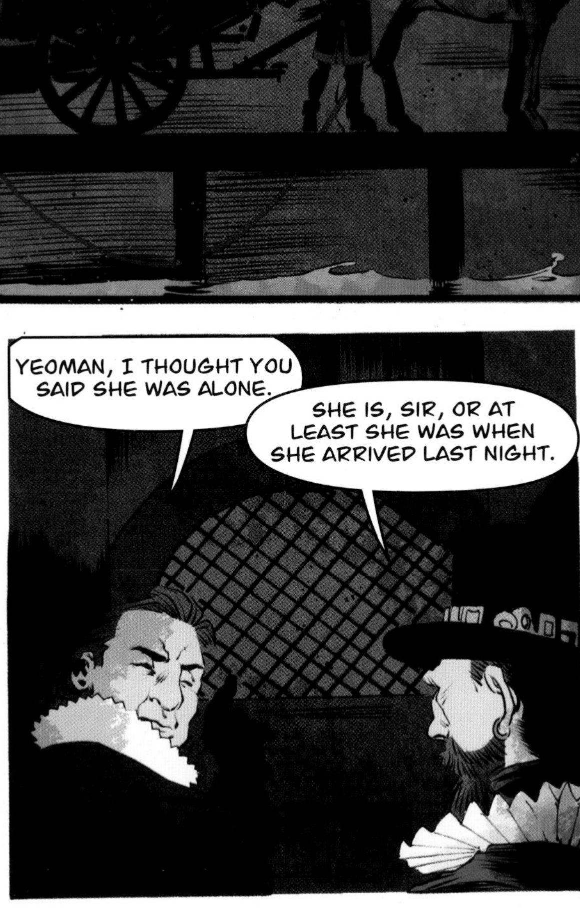
YEOMAN, I THOUGHT YOU SAID SHE WAS ALONE.
SHE IS, SIR, OR AT LEAST SHE WAS WHEN SHE ARRIVED LAST NIGHT.

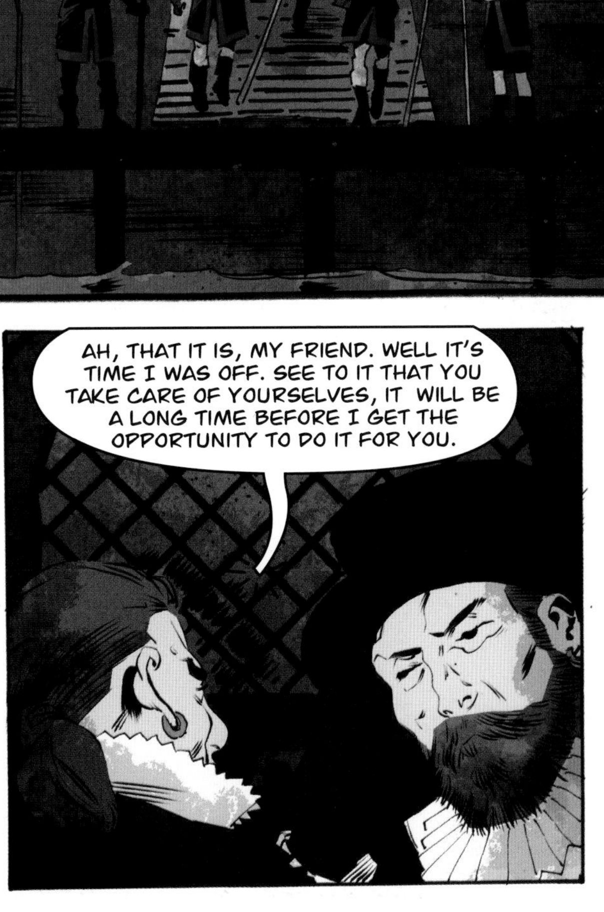
AH, THAT IT IS, MY FRIEND. WELL IT'S TIME I WAS OFF. SEE TO IT THAT YOU TAKE CARE OF YOURSELVES, IT WILL BE A LONG TIME BEFORE I GET THE OPPORTUNITY TO DO IT FOR YOU.

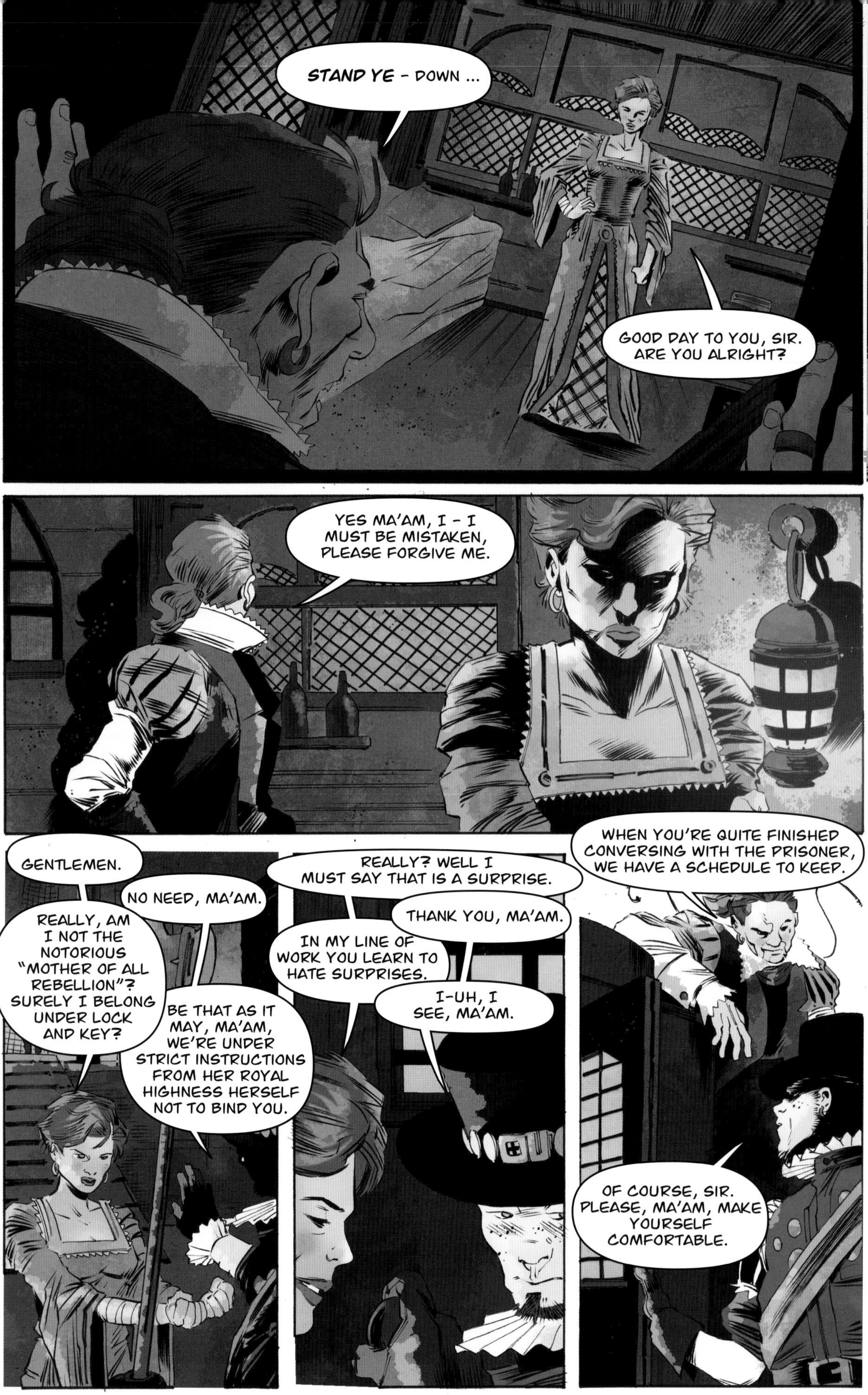
STAND YE - DOWN ...
GOOD DAY TO YOU, SIR. ARE YOU ALRIGHT?
YES MA'AM, I - I MUST BE MISTAKEN, PLEASE FORGIVE ME.
GENTLEMEN.
REALLY, AM I NOT THE NOTORIOUS "MOTHER OF ALL REBELLION"? SURELY I BELONG UNDER LOCK AND KEY?
NO NEED, MA'AM.
BE THAT AS IT MAY, MA'AM, WE'RE UNDER STRICT INSTRUCTIONS FROM HER ROYAL HIGHNESS HERSELF NOT TO BIND YOU.
REALLY? WELL I MUST SAY THAT IS A SURPRISE.
IN MY LINE OF WORK YOU LEARN TO HATE SURPRISES.
THANK YOU, MA'AM.
I-UH, I SEE, MA'AM.
WHEN YOU'RE QUITE FINISHED CONVERSING WITH THE PRISONER, WE HAVE A SCHEDULE TO KEEP.
OF COURSE, SIR. PLEASE, MA'AM, MAKE YOURSELF COMFORTABLE.

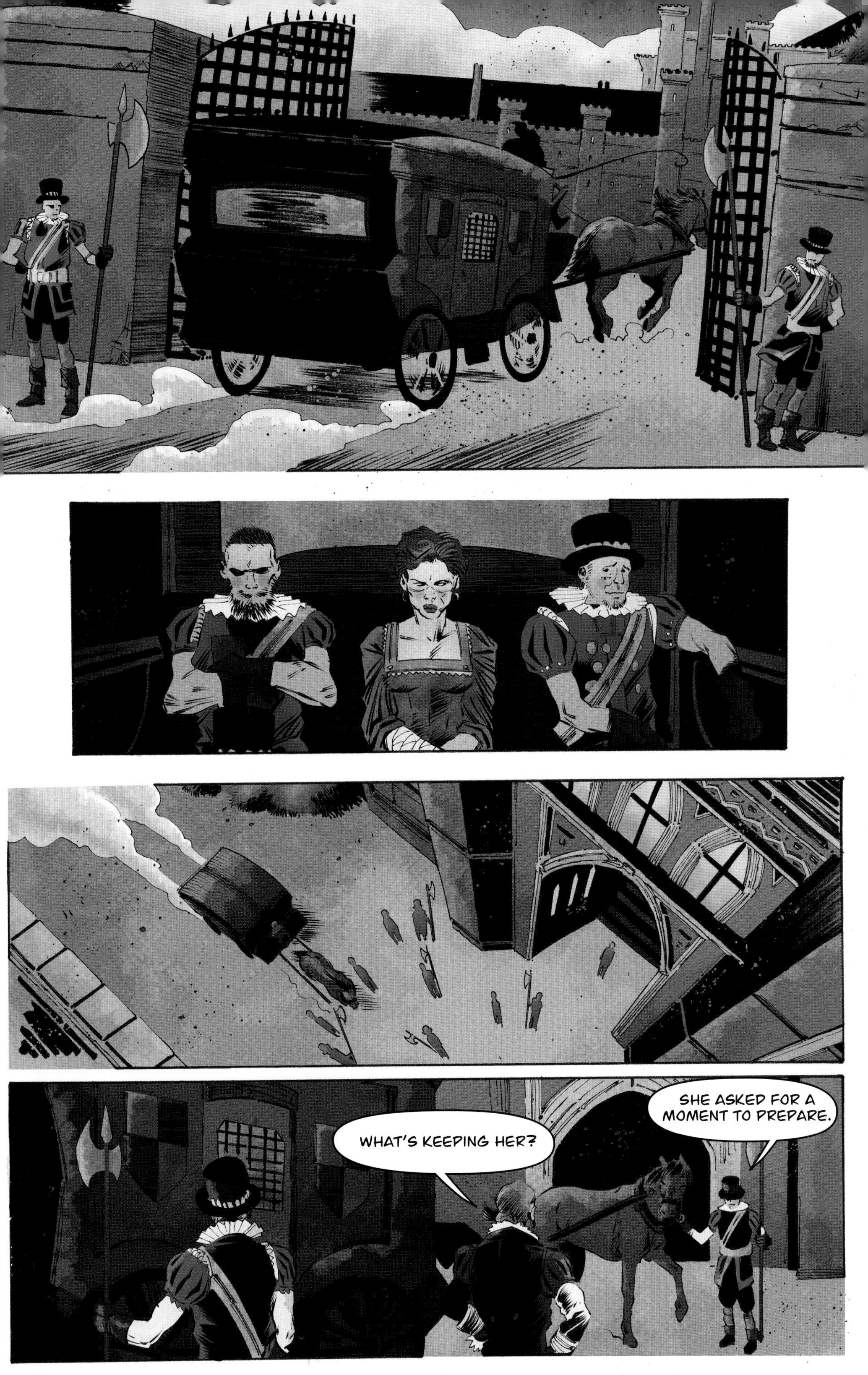
WHAT'S KEEPING HER?
SHE ASKED FOR A MOMENT TO PREPARE.

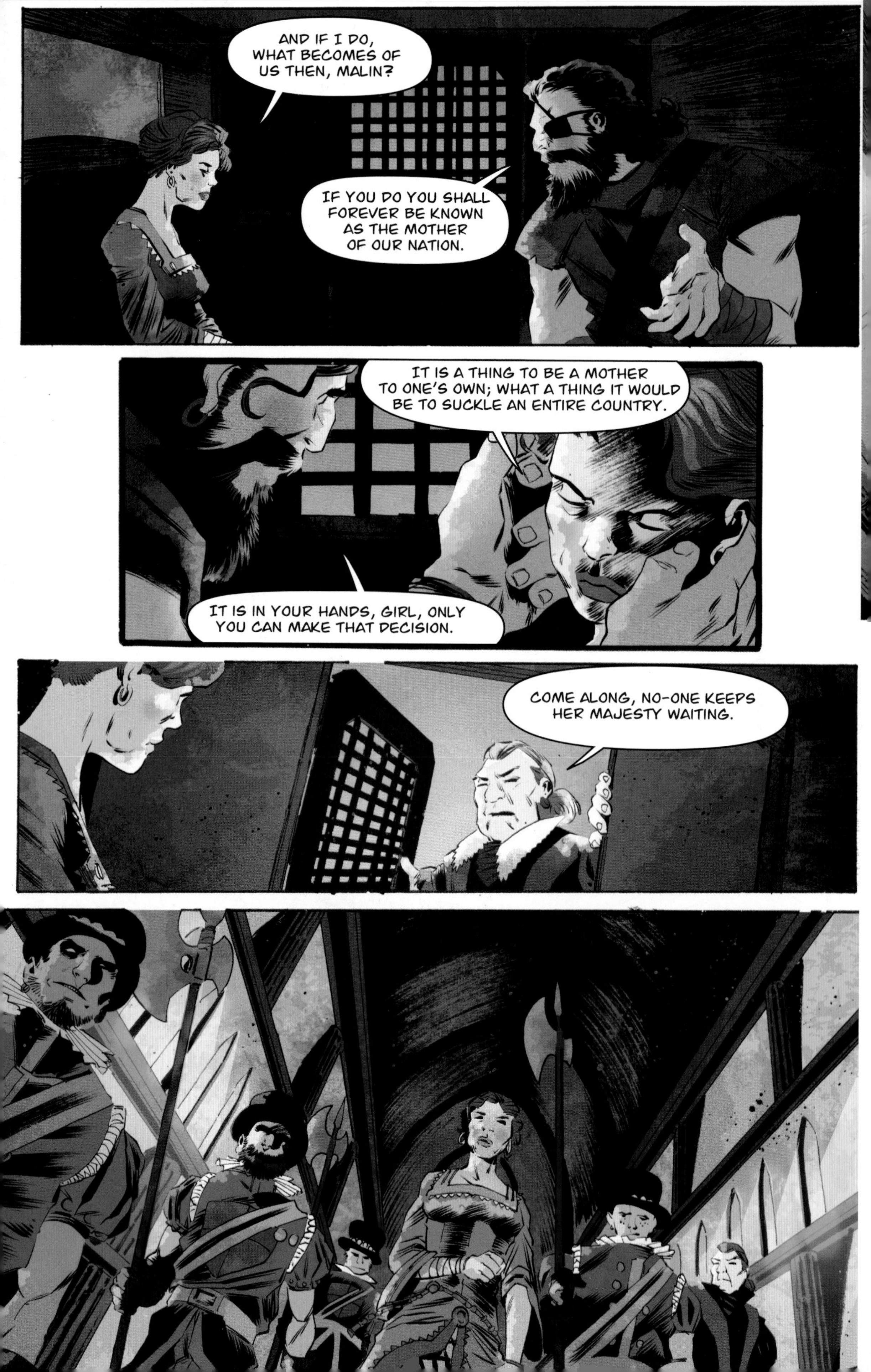
AND IF I DO, WHAT BECOMES OF US THEN, MALIN?
IF YOU DO YOU SHALL FOREVER BE KNOWN AS THE MOTHER OF OUR NATION.
IT IS A THING TO BE A MOTHER TO ONE'S OWN; WHAT A THING IT WOULD BE TO SUCKLE AN ENTIRE COUNTRY.
IT IS IN YOUR HANDS, GIRL, ONLY YOU CAN MAKE THAT DECISION.
COME ALONG, NO-ONE KEEPS HER MAJESTY WAITING.

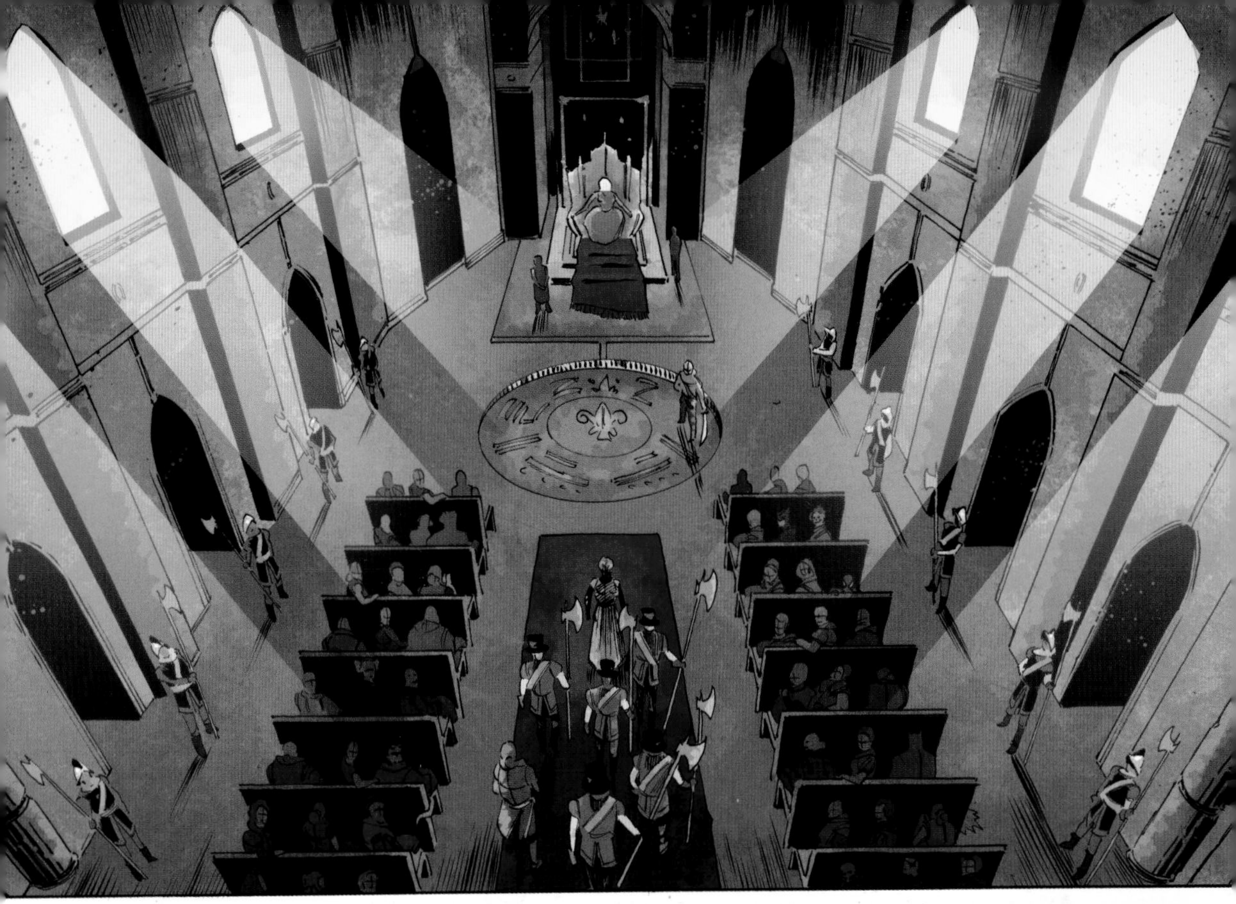

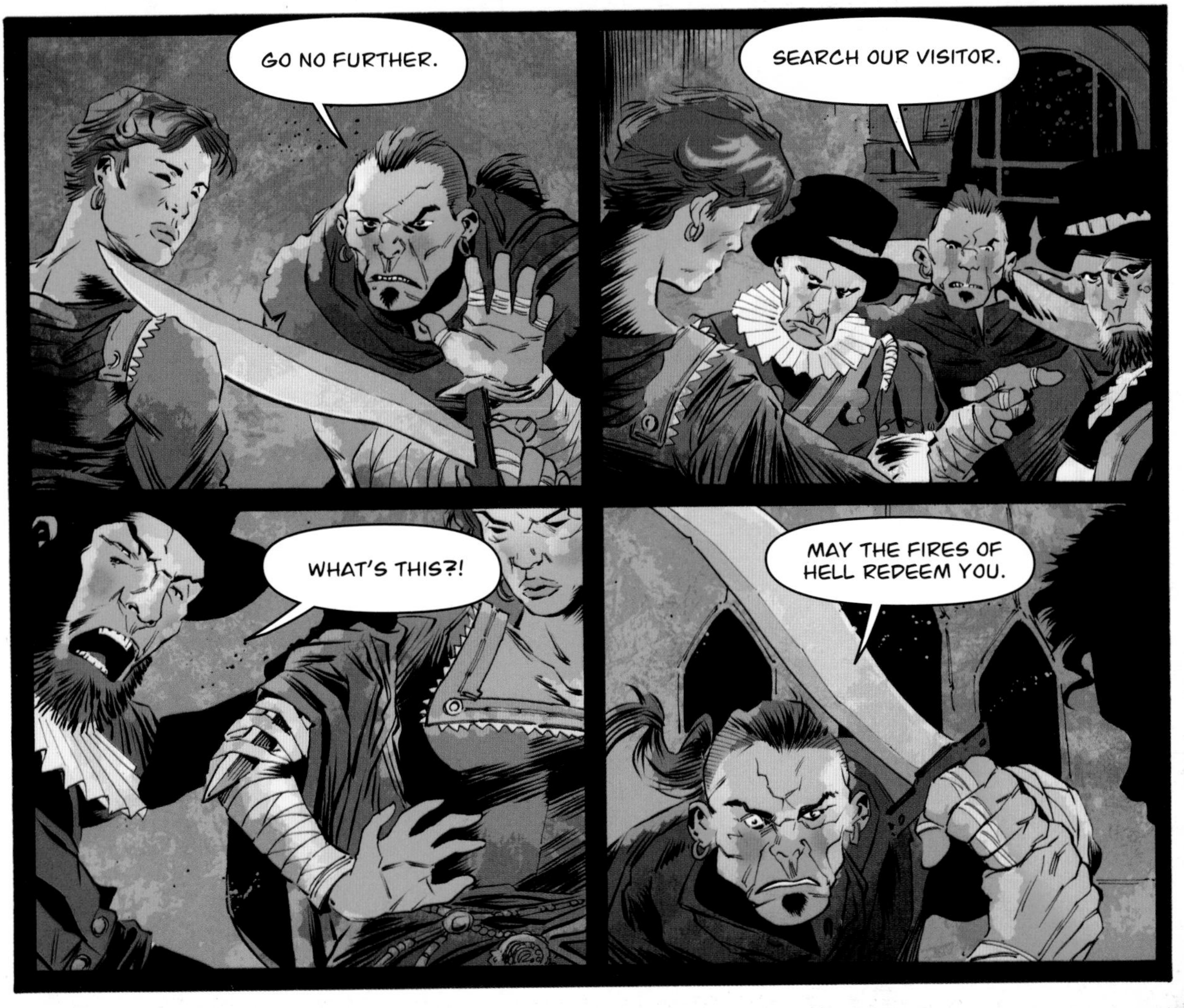
GO NO FURTHER.
SEARCH OUR VISITOR.
WHAT'S THIS?!
MAY THE FIRES OF HELL REDEEM YOU.

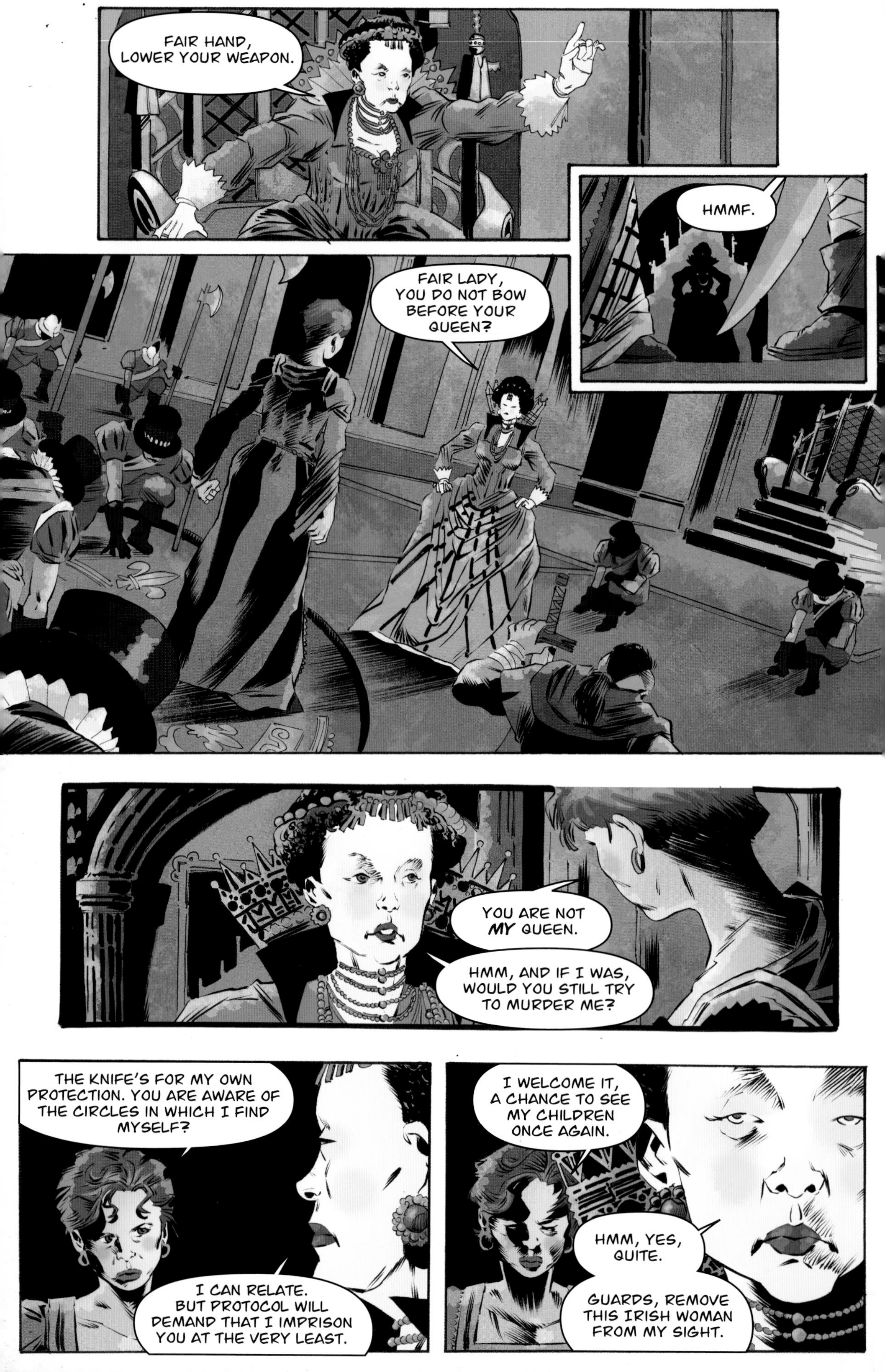
FAIR HAND, LOWER YOUR WEAPON.
HMMF.
FAIR LADY, YOU DO NOT BOW BEFORE YOUR QUEEN?
YOU ARE NOT *MY* QUEEN.
HMM, AND IF I WAS, WOULD YOU STILL TRY TO MURDER ME?
THE KNIFE'S FOR MY OWN PROTECTION. YOU ARE AWARE OF THE CIRCLES IN WHICH I FIND MYSELF?
I CAN RELATE. BUT PROTOCOL WILL DEMAND THAT I IMPRISON YOU AT THE VERY LEAST.
I WELCOME IT, A CHANCE TO SEE MY CHILDREN ONCE AGAIN.
HMM, YES, QUITE.
GUARDS, REMOVE THIS IRISH WOMAN FROM MY SIGHT.

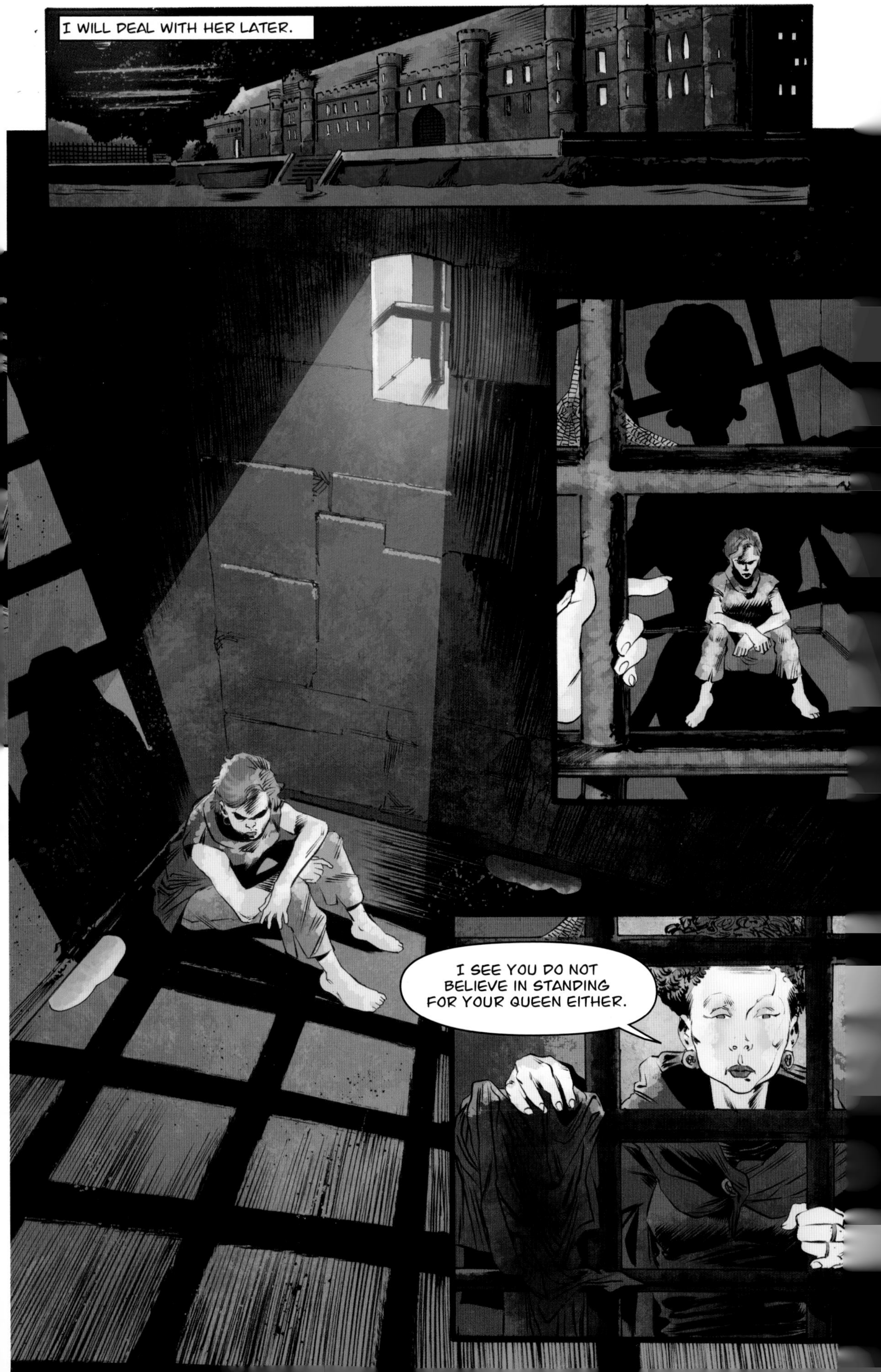
I WILL DEAL WITH HER LATER.
I SEE YOU DO NOT BELIEVE IN STANDING FOR YOUR QUEEN EITHER.

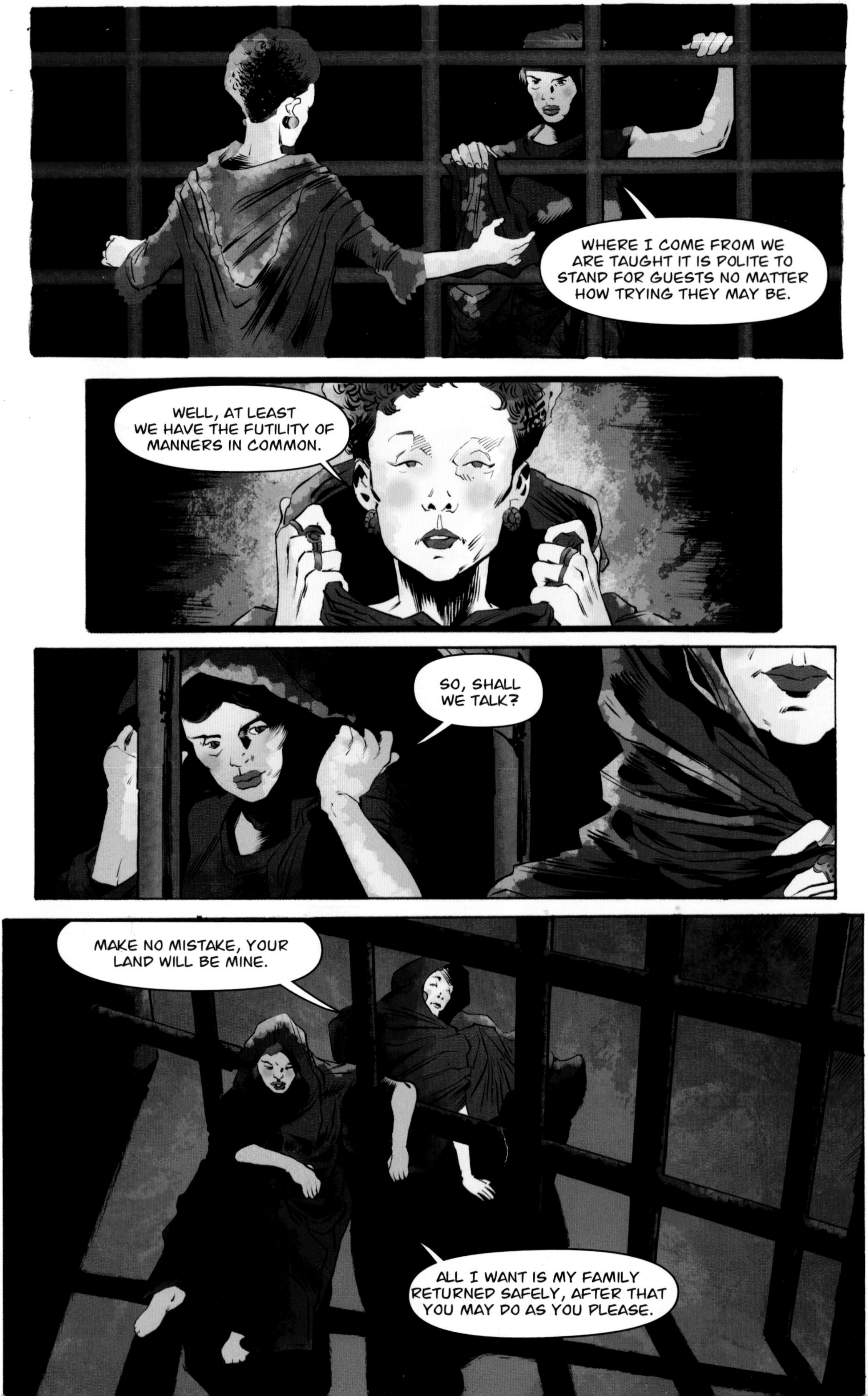
WHERE I COME FROM WE ARE TAUGHT IT IS POLITE TO STAND FOR GUESTS NO MATTER HOW TRYING THEY MAY BE.
WELL, AT LEAST WE HAVE THE FUTILITY OF MANNERS IN COMMON.
SO, SHALL WE TALK?
MAKE NO MISTAKE, YOUR LAND WILL BE MINE.
ALL I WANT IS MY FAMILY RETURNED SAFELY, AFTER THAT YOU MAY DO AS YOU PLEASE.

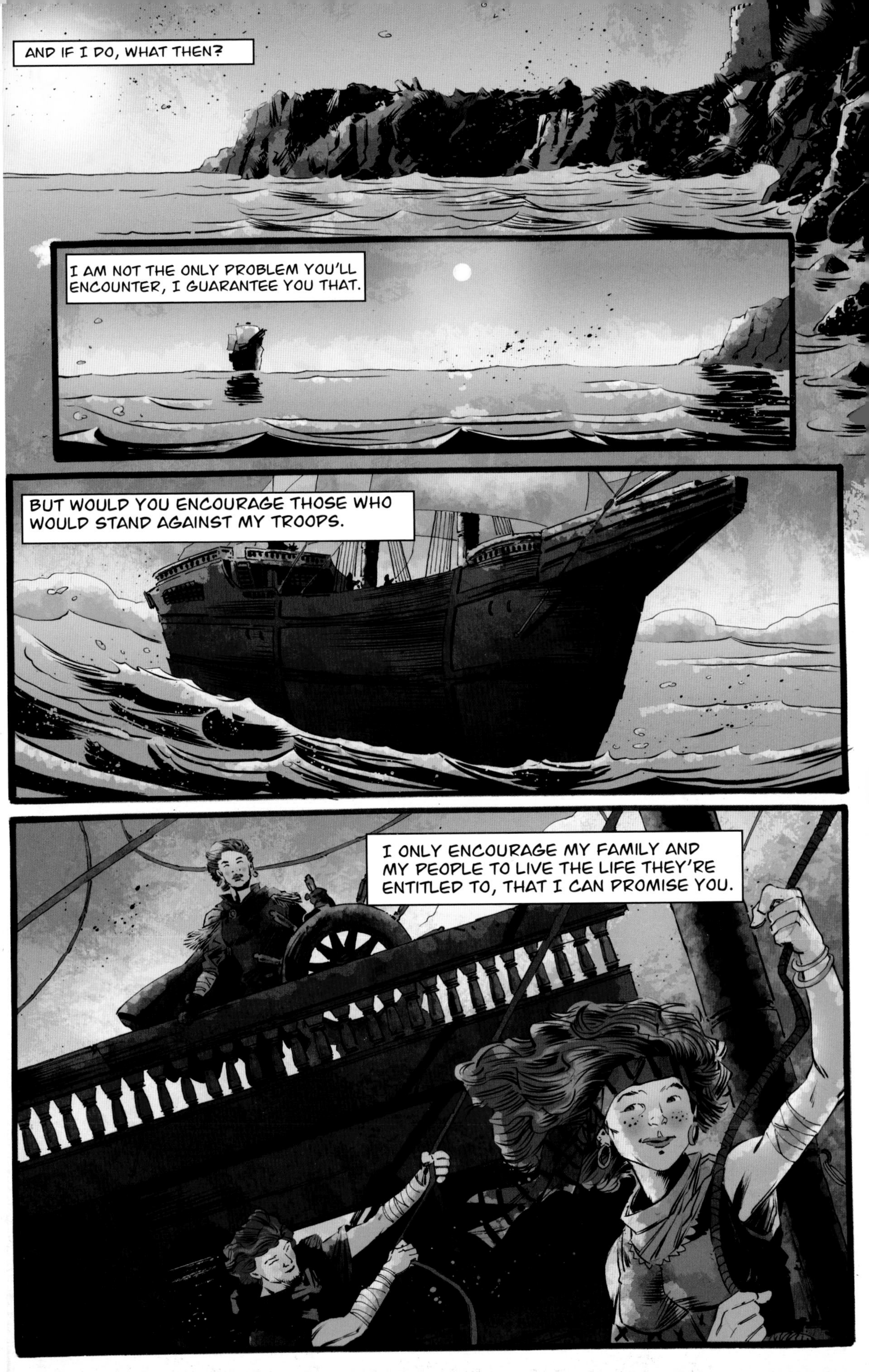
AND IF I DO, WHAT THEN?
I AM NOT THE ONLY PROBLEM YOU'LL ENCOUNTER, I GUARANTEE YOU THAT.
BUT WOULD YOU ENCOURAGE THOSE WHO WOULD STAND AGAINST MY TROOPS.
I ONLY ENCOURAGE MY FAMILY AND MY PEOPLE TO LIVE THE LIFE THEY'RE ENTITLED TO, THAT I CAN PROMISE YOU.

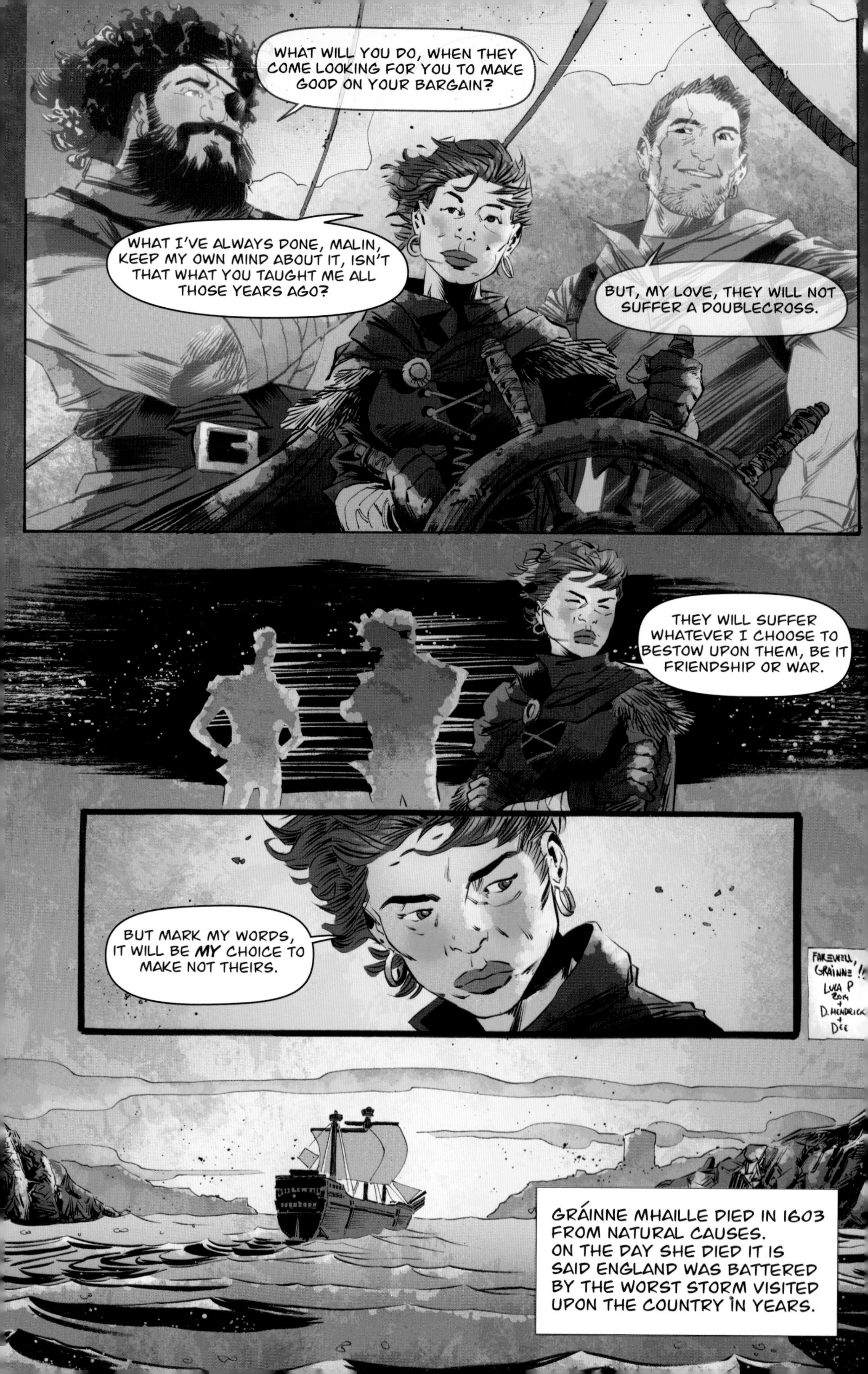
WHAT WILL YOU DO, WHEN THEY COME LOOKING FOR YOU TO MAKE GOOD ON YOUR BARGAIN?
WHAT I'VE ALWAYS DONE, MALIN, KEEP MY OWN MIND ABOUT IT, ISN'T THAT WHAT YOU TAUGHT ME ALL THOSE YEARS AGO?
BUT, MY LOVE, THEY WILL NOT SUFFER A DOUBLECROSS.
THEY WILL SUFFER WHATEVER I CHOOSE TO BESTOW UPON THEM, BE IT FRIENDSHIP OR WAR.
BUT MARK MY WORDS, IT WILL BE *MY* CHOICE TO MAKE NOT THEIRS.
FAREWELL, GRÁINNE!! LUCA P 2014 + D. HENDRICK + DEE
GRÁINNE MHAILLE DIED IN 1603 FROM NATURAL CAUSES. ON THE DAY SHE DIED IT IS SAID ENGLAND WAS BATTERED BY THE WORST STORM VISITED UPON THE COUNTRY IN YEARS.

GRANUAILE
Queen of Storms

Granuaile, the pirate queen, was a real historical figure who lived in six-teenth century Ireland. Known by the English version of her name, Grace O'Malley, the Irish, Gráinne Ní Mháille, or the nickname, Granuaile, she was the daughter of Eoghan O'Malley, a chieftain from Connacht, on the west coast of Ireland. After his death she took over as chieftain, running the clan business – which was nominally sea trading and shipping, but was also said to involve piracy and the payment of 'protection money' to ships passing through her waters.

She married Domhnall O'Flaherty (known as 'Domhnall an Choghaidh' or 'Domhnall of the Battles'), whose family ruled Iar-Connacht (mod-ern-day Connemara) and they had three children together, Eoghan, Margaret and Murrough. After Domhnall's death, she married Richard Burke, of Rockfleet Castle, Co. Mayo. Legend has it that she married him for his castle and holdings and divorced him, in accordance with Brehon law, after a single year. It's said that she retained control of Rockfleet, and the sea around it where pirate ships could hide. Gráinne and Richard Bourke had one son together, Tibbot na Long ('Tibbot of the ships').

Granuaile really did have an audience with Queen Elizabeth I of England. By the late sixteenth century, English rule in Ireland was encroaching fur-ther west; after several of Gráinne's family members were taken captive by Sir Richard Bingham, the English governor of Connacht, she sailed to London to meet with the queen. The two women conversed together in Latin, face to face, as two great leaders.

Granuaile died in around 1603. Many locations in Connacht, Clare Island, Rockfleet and Westport House, have connections to Granuaile and can still be visited today.

First published 2015 by
The O'Brien Press Ltd,
12 Terenure Road East, Rathgar,
Dublin 6, Ireland.
Tel: +353 1 4923333; Fax: +353 1 4922777
E-mail: books@obrien.ie.
Website: www.obrien.ie
ISBN: 978-1-84717-671-4
Text © copyright Dave Hendrick 2015
Copyright for illustration, typesetting, layout, editing, design
© Luca Pizzari
Colouring: Dee Cunniffe
Lettering: Peter Marry
Cover title text design: Peter Marry

8 7 6 5 4 3 2 1
19 18 17 16 15

Printed and bound in Poland by Białostockie Zakłady Graficzne S.A.
The paper in this book is produced using pulp from managed forests

The O'Brien Press receives financial assistance from